# The Cutting Edge of Wallpaper

black dog
publishing

# Contents

6 *A Papered History*
by Timothy Brittain-Catlin

18 *The New Wallpaper*
by Jane Audas

26 *DECORATIVE*

Louise Body 30
Manuel Canovas 32
Cole & Son 34
Neisha Crosland 36
Linda Florence 38
Fromental 40
Jane Gordon Clark 44
Hemingway Design 46
The Magnificent Chatwin Brothers 48
Timorous Beasties 50
Twenty2 54
Erica Wakerly 56

58 *FIGURATIVE*

Absolute Zero° 62
Lizzie Allen 64
Birgit Amadori 66
Deborah Bowness 68
Erotic Dragon 70
Nama Rococo 72
Nice 74
Ten and Don 76
William Wegman 78
Hanna Werning 80
Wook Kim 84

88 *ABSTRACT AND GEOMETRIC*

Johanna Basford 92
Basso & Brooke 94
Markus Benesch 98
Committee 100
Dominic Crinson 102
Dan Funderburgh 104
Jane Masters 108
Virgil Marti 110
Jorge Pardo 112
PSYOP 114
Showroom Dummies 116

118 *ARCHITECTURAL*

Heather Barnett 122
Susan Bradley 126
Clare Coles 128
Front 132
Tracy Kendall 134
Ross Neil 138
Maria Yaschuk 140

142 *INTERACTIVE*

Antoine et Manuel 146
Blik 148
Simon Heijdens 150
Ich&Kar 154
Rachel Kelly 156
Lene Toni Kjeld 158
Christopher Pearson 160
Pepper-mint 162
Jenny Wilkinson 164

166 *Wallpaper as Art: a brief history*
by Charles Stuckey

174 *Bibliography*

175 *Acknowledgements*

# A Papered History
## Timothy Brittain-Catlin

To cover a wall with wallpaper is to open up a window onto an ideal world. The idea is simple: you can capture an image from anywhere you please, and transfer it onto the walls of your own home. But the simplicity of the idea hides a complicated story, which involves a remarkable range of possibilities. Paper can imitate fabrics, marbles, woods, leathers, metals and tiles, as well as realistic botanical and natural subjects. Patterns can play along with the architecture of a room, or they can disguise it; they can be geometrical and repetitive, or they can simply be one-off illustrations that transform a room into a picture gallery. To choose a paper for the room you like to inhabit is to make a statement about how you see yourself, and how you want to see the world.

The story of wallpaper is one that combines the search for accessible and pleasant forms with the process of technical advance; changing the relationships homeowners have with their homes. What a wallpaper is for, who chooses it, who pays for it, who applies it and who appreciates it are all questions that have had different answers at different times. The very fact that there have been long stretches in the history of the domestic interior—most notably, between the two World Wars—when wallpaper was almost entirely absent from fashionable interiors is itself a sign that decorators and design critics considered it to be a significant part of a room. In 1938, the *Amt der Schönheit der Arbeit* or 'Office for the Beauty of Work' of the German Reich dictated 25 designs for wallpaper that henceforth were to be produced by all manufacturers throughout the country.[1] Although no comparison can be made between that situation and the invasiveness of our present day arbiters of taste, it was an episode that emphasised the fact that the way in which we choose to decorate the walls of our homes is a strong personal statement, which may or not be acceptable to others. Indeed, those who have wanted to reform the home have often aimed at changing our wallpaper—often the cheapest and the easiest way of transforming a whole room.

### The Early History of Wallpaper

The earliest wallpapers in England were individual sheets, decorated with geometrical woodcut patterns and printed in black ink on pale paper by a hand-operated press in the same way as the leaves of a book; sometimes they were hand coloured. Fragments of some of these early sheets have survived: they can be dated back as far as the late sixteenth century to the mercantile boom and busy urban growth that characterised the reign of Queen Elizabeth. Framed patterns, perhaps 30 centimetres square, could be pasted together on a ceiling to imitate coffering. They could have been used for everything from covering up an unfortunate space, masking uneven plasterwork or as an innovative alternative to hanging pictures on the wall.

As printing and publishing grew, so did wallpaper: the sale of wallpaper was then associated with the stationery business.

*Fruit Wallpaper*, designed by William Morris, printed using woodblocks, by Jeffrey & Co, 1886.

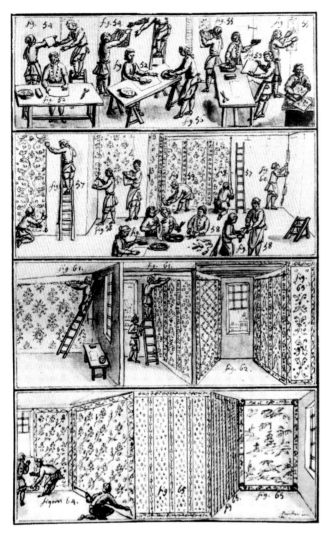

Drawing illustrating
methods of paper-hanging;
mid-eighteenth century,
JM Papillon (1698–1776),
private collection.

Papers might be used for lining boxes as well as for decorating the walls of a room. Towards the end of the seventeenth century London had become a centre for wallpapers, sold at a wide range of prices to reflect the trouble taken in their manufacture and the extent to which they reflected popular fashion.

These late seventeenth century papers had repeating, often floral, patterns, but were otherwise different from papers sold today that imitate their styles. Known as 'paper hangings', they were often seen as a direct substitute for fabrics, and could be pinned rather than glued with flour and water paste onto the walls. A further difference was due to the block printing process, which required every printed sheet to have a selvedge (a blank margin) on both sides. One or both of these selvedges could be trimmed off by the paperhanger; frequently, however, the margins were simply covered by a border, with the result that the room appeared to have been divided up into paper panels. The possibility of a matching or contrasting border naturally enhanced the attractiveness of papering a wall, creating an effect which was truly derived from the papering itself rather than anything else, even the applied borders were themselves printed in the form of increasingly realistic tassels and fabric swags. In this way, the modern idea of a wallpapered interior was born: no longer was a paper chosen simply to look attractive as a pasted object on a wall—from now on, the overall effect of the finished room was considered at the outset.

## English Papers up to the Nineteenth Century

By the middle of the eighteenth century England had become a centre of technical innovation in wallpaper manufacture: sheets were pasted together to form rolls before printing, allowing a larger repeat pattern. This was aesthetically significant as it soon led to a type of paper that had an even and regular effect, well suited to the covering of all the walls of a room. English designers soon began to establish a series of design innovations for wallpaper, which were embraced by design communities around the world.

The floral patterns from this period that exploit the roll lengths already begin to look familiar to modern eyes. But the English wallpaper trade established other precedents too. One of these was the arrival of papers designated for different types of room—red for dining rooms, green for private picture galleries (because it contrasted well with gilt frames), and so on. Another was the appearance of flock, probably towards the end of the seventeenth century and well developed by the 1730s. Flock was made from dyed woollen waste which was glued in large, stylised floral patterns onto backing paper already printed with a similar colour, creating an effect similar to that of damask: the striking contrast of surviving papers of this era is due to the fading pigments in the paper itself. A third was a thriving market in cheap, geometrical papers that could transform any room, at a reasonable price.

The earliest surviving papers were generally printed in black on white; the Victoria and Albert Museum in London has an example from Kingston upon Thames of about 1680 where the single pigment is employed to remarkable effect in an imitation of lace. It seems likely that more ambitious colour effects followed the desire by manufacturers to imitate fashionable luxury products that were imported from abroad. From the mid-seventeenth century, for example, the English became enthusiastic importers of Chinese papers, which were actually hand-painted, customised murals rather than printed hangings. Imitating such a colourful effect by block printing, however, would have been time consuming and expensive. Most commercial papers were given a coat of background colour by hand, and then printed with contrasting distempers. Some manufacturers combined printing with stencilling and other techniques; but in general, the extent to which wallpapers could imitate the complex colouring of tapestries or needlepoint was severely limited. The result was again that wallpaper designs had to find their own distinct language. One popular style from the mid-eighteenth century was architectural paper, for example a bold motif in the form of an aedicule known as a 'pillar and arch' pattern. Like most surviving papers of the period—those for the most part to be found preserved under subsequent layers—these usually employed only two or three colours.

Whilst the English led the way in the production of mechanical papers with busy, repetitive designs, French manufacturers of the later eighteenth century employed well paid artists to design papers, known as *papiers peints*, which were intended as luxury items for a small market. The best-known name in the French industry, Jean-Baptiste Réveillon, was well established before the French Revolution of 1789. The best French manufacturers specialised in creating individual panels, free-standing architectural devices for large rooms sometimes taking the form of unfolding narratives based on Classical (or Napoleonic) epics. These designs were characteristically highly realistic botanical or architectural illustrations, and employed expensive, newly available pigments or luxury finishes such as gold dust. A series of time-consuming visual effects were introduced: these included *Irisé*, a method of achieving subtle graduations in colour. A large number of blocks—occasionally as many as 4,000—required considerable expertise in scheduling and timing the printing process.[2]

## Mechanisation and Experimentation

The arrival of steam-driven surface roller printing in the early nineteenth century, pioneered by Potter & Co of Darwen in Lancashire, led to the possibility of multi-coloured papers at accessible prices; at first, however, these rollers did not allow for delicate detailing, and the speedy process and thinner inks often resulted in slightly blurry or indistinct prints.

Sheet of wallpaper with formalised floral design on lattice-patterned ground, English, late seventeenth century, woodblock print.

*The Sleeping Beauty*,
1879, by Walter Crane
(1845–1915), produced
by Jeffrey & Co, colour
machine print.

By 1850, however, it was possible to print eight different colours perfectly registered; the new visual potential of wallpaper, combined with the fact that tax on paper was finally removed altogether in 1861, resulted in a huge increase in manufacturing output. According to Joanna Banham, in 1834 about 1.2 million rolls a year were produced Britain; in 1874 the figure was 32 million.[3]

From the 1850s, perhaps as a result of the display of eye-catching wallpaper designs at the Crystal Palace and at subsequent exhibitions, British manufacturers such as William Woollams and Jeffrey & Co began to compete with the French luxury papers; others experimented as much with a variety of textures as with the actual designs themselves. The use of arsenic, for creating a shade of green, in wallpaper was outlawed, thus removing the lingering suspicion that it could be dangerous in situations such as bedrooms. Washable papers, known as 'hygienic' or 'sanitary' papers, had varnished or lacquered surfaces making them suitable for bathrooms or other exposed areas. Furthermore, these were expressly marketed at the most modest of households, but without the kinds of designs thought suitable by critics and design reformers for those in need of a lesson in good taste. In fact the late nineteenth century launched a whole series of experimental textures and finishes. Frederick Walton, the inventor of linoleum, devised an embossed paper with a similar composition called Lincrusta Walton in 1877; and Anaglypta, a cheaper product made of cotton fibre pulp, appeared nine years later.

Whilst upmarket designers imitated embossed leather with designs that were described as 'Spanish', or 'silk velvet', mass producers embarked on a series of entirely new textures unique to wallpaper. As a general rule, the colours of the papers produced for the mass market in Britain became indistinct and porridge-like; creative effort seems still to have been directed largely at experimenting with new surfaces, in particular hardwearing ones that would supersede the Victorian washable papers that carried connotations of poverty. Various methods of embossing were tried out; woodchip paper, which masks uneven plaster finishes, first made its appearance in the 1930s. Plastics began to emerge with the revival of the use of wallpaper after the Second World War; Vymura, a paper with a washable vinyl surface, appeared in 1961. The arrival of artificial flock coincided with the spread of Indian restaurants, creating the famously indissoluble link between the two; ironically, flock had been thought unsuitable for dining rooms when originally introduced 250 years beforehand because it tended to absorb and retain the smell of food. Finally, new printing processes including mechanised screenprinting and photogravure also made their mark. By the end of the twentieth century, wallpaper could technically do just about anything.

## Wallpaper Revolutionaries 1: AWN Pugin

There have been two wallpaper designers who have left
an indelible mark on the history of the design and use of
wallpaper in Britain over the last 150 years: AWN Pugin
in the early years of the reign of Queen Victoria; and Laura
Ashley in the 1980s. Both of these two were unusual and also
profoundly religious characters; both seem to have been
highly regarded within the artistic establishment—indeed,
increasingly so after their early deaths—and yet at the same
time much derided by those who write about the middle
market tastes they both set out to conquer. In both cases,
they tapped into central questions about what the design
of a domestic interior is actually for, and left behind them
a completely transformed professional world.

The son of a successful French *émigré* designer and
draughtsman who lived at the centre of a lively artistic circle
in Bloomsbury, Pugin was a precocious artist as a child.
His unparalleled knowledge of mediaeval design was
well-employed during his time as draughtsman for Charles
Barry's winning scheme for the Houses of Parliament in
1835. Yet Pugin originally made his reputation as a polemical
writer and illustrator rather than as a designer. His first
book, *Contrasts*, of 1836, was an attack on the nastiness and
cheapness of modern design; his second, *The True Principles
of Pointed or Christian Architecture*, of 1841, consists of a series
of clear instructions to architects, explaining how exactly
they should deal with every aspect of the design of a building.
The most important of the 'true principles' themselves are laid
out at the very start of the book; there are to be "no features
about a building which are not necessary for convenience,
construction, or propriety"; and secondly, "all ornament
should consist of enrichment of the essential construction
of the building".[4] The rest of the book is then taken up with
explanations of how mediaeval architects followed these
principles, and how modern designers ought to start again
along these lines, a process which according to Pugin
necessarily required revisiting Gothic architecture.

Pugin was not alone in campaigning for a rational,
methodical way of building, but he was certainly unique in the
way he went about it—both in his engaging style of writing,
and also in the sense of moral purpose that he attached to the
act of construction. He was also unique in his ability to design
in a way that demonstrated his 'principles', an ability that
stretched as far as wallpaper. On page 26 of *The True Principles*
he included an impressive bicolour block print of a design
for a flock wallpaper, which like other of his designs appears
to have been derived from sixteenth century North European
patterns for damask rather than from the earlier medieval
designs of which he generally approved. This is contrasted
with a caricature of a wallpaper of his time, in this case a
'Modern Gothic Paper' consisting of a series of gothic
aedicules, shaded as if in perspective, and framing a vignette

Chintz-style wallpaper,
with matching border;
English, late eighteenth
century, colour
woodblock print.

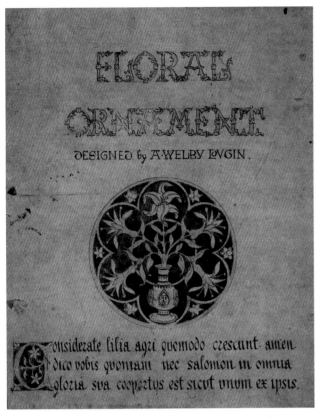

The title page for the 1849 edition of *Floral Ornament*.

of a fountain in a garden. Pugin remarked that this latter type of paper is "a great favourite with hotel and tavern keepers"; it was ridiculous not only because of the ornate nature of the image but also because of the employment of perspectival shading in the design.[5] Much contemporary wallpaper, gothic or not, architectural or floral, used shading; and, as Pugin maintains, with absurd result, as it repeats "a perspective over a large surface with some hundred different points of sight"; in fact, of course, there are an infinite number.

Pugin's proposed design therefore completely avoided naturalistic forms, which would require shading in order for them to be legible. But it did a great deal more than that. In the first place, it formed part of a lesson in designing everything in accordance with the material from which it is made; timber roofs, for example, are to be constructed as they were in medieval times in accordance with the natural properties of timber. A flat material requires a flat pattern; and so the artist's job is to extract some essential characteristic that can be rendered in two dimensions from the natural forms he wants to copy. The exercise of developing new flat depictions of natural forms intrigued him, and in 1849 he produced an entire book of designs like this called *Floral Ornament*; these could be easily reproduced, for example as stencil patterns in a new church. His papers were mainly produced for the interior designer John Crace by Samuel Scott & Co in Islington and the blocks are still in use today. His most memorable designs are probably those based around adaptations of heraldic symbols, their authentic medieval origins being particularly suitable for application to carved wooden blocks.

For Pugin, wallpaper had an important role to play in the creation of a new type of domestic interior: he seemed to believe that it was a moral imperative for an architect to control every detail of an interior. No other contemporary prescriptive writer on domestic architecture, such as Alfred Bartholomew or John Loudon, gave wallpaper the prominence he did. Furthermore, it would have been significant for an aspiring designer to see that Pugin's wallpaper pattern-making fitted neatly into a coherent family with designs for the other crafts of the Gothic Revival, such as encaustic tiles, gold and silverware formed from flat sheets of metals, or even stained glass.[6] After the great public success of the Great Exhibition of 1851 where he presented a 'Medieval Court' designed entirely by himself, it became clear to many people that here was a fresh new approach to wallpaper that could be copied in middle class homes, unlike the extremely expensive, one-off multi block French designs exhibited elsewhere. But far beyond Pugin's own immediate influence was the fact that his approach was almost at once taken up by influential designers.

Owen Jones, a designer for the Exhibition, published *The Grammar of Ornament* in 1856. This book, which illustrated a vast range of designs including many from various non-European cultures, was republished nine times before 1910, including an American edition of 1880, which was later used by Frank Lloyd Wright.[7] Jones' preface listed 37 propositions concerning "general principles in the arrangement of form and colour, in architecture and the decorative arts": the first of these was the Puginian statement that "the decorative arts arise from, and should properly be attendant upon, architecture". He then continued to list ways in which the decoration should be generated on natural or geometrical lines, and gave some detailed instructions, for example, that "primary colours should be used on the upper portions of objects, the secondary and tertiary on the lower". The designs were mainly of the kind that could be easily and cheaply reproduced on a flat surface; so much so, that in fact Jones' *Grammar* seems today almost to be a kind of pattern book for wallpaper.

## Design Reform

Jones was part of a movement known as 'Design Reform', which believed, in the words of his concluding proposition, that "no improvement can take place in the Art of the present generation until all classes, artists, manufacturers and the public, are better educated in art, and the existence of general principles is more fully recognised". On the one hand, a statement like this is a sign that the early nineteenth century principle of positivism, the tendency to see all things as being classifiable, had finally penetrated into the details of interior decoration. On the other, it also provides a clear example of the contemporary process towards governmentalisation, the process by which more and more aspects of life were governed by the state and its bureaucracies: Jones, like his patron Sir Henry Cole, were state employees and they believed explicitly in the role of the state in promoting good design in humble households.

Design Reform as a political movement was in a sense the older brother of one of the very few English artistic movements ever to make an impact outside of the: the later Victorian Arts and Crafts movement, which was characterised by a Puginian belief that all human existence must be remade through artistic craftsmanship. Its disciples believed that designers must themselves physically create new objects, utterly rejecting the machine, along with most of the economic practicalities of life. The most famous of all the designers of the movement, William Morris, was himself influenced by Jones; with his startling ability to turn his hand to every aspect of hand-crafted applied design, he also became an enthusiastic designer of wallpaper. He made something in the region of 50 designs over a period of about 30 years, starting with his *Trellis* design of 1862.[8] From 1864 the papers of Morris, Marshall, Faulkner & Co were made by Jeffrey & Co, who were already producing Jones' work. Morris' designs were quite different from either Pugin's or Jones': he achieved the difficult goal of merging the geometrical, essentially two-dimensional, designs which met Pugin's criteria for

Section of a classical 'pillar and arch' wallpaper; English, Chiaroscuro woodblock print, c 1769.

Wallpaper with formalised foliage design, colour woodblock print, mid-nineteenthth century, by Owen James, 1809–1874.

## The modern trend

Interior decoration today makes effective use of bold and colourful patterns in contrast with plain surfaces of pastel shade. This charming bedroom is an excellent example of modern practice.

*Crown*
WALLPAPERS
*best in the world*
The Wall Paper Manufacturers Limited

Crown Wallpapers advertisement, 1951.

wallpaper with much more naturalistic detailing. *Trellis*, for example, featured birds drawn by his loyal friend, the architect Philip Webb. By the early 1870s, Morris had become proficient in the design of intense, swirling patterns in which a background pattern of dense foliage characteristically merges with the flowers in the foreground; the very subtle use of comparatively few colours, rigorously enforced by Morris who insisted on the highest standards of production, has resulted in papers that have enjoyed popularity almost continuously to this day, being manufactured now by Sanderson who took over the designs on the demise of Jeffrey & Co in 1925.

Both Morris and Webb seem to have preferred hanging these papers on a wall where they would contrast with the fresh white paintwork of the ceiling and joinery; their high class clients, on the other hand, preferred them as merely one of a riotous assembly of colours and shapes, including on the ceilings of rooms, creating an effect Morris described as similar to being inside a box.[9] At all events, in early days they provided a battleground for those with aesthetic tastes on the one side, and those who preferred more conservative treatments on the other. By its association first with Pugin and his moral crusade for revolutionary design, secondly with the design reformers of the South Kensington (now Victoria and Albert) Museum, and finally with Morris' all-embracing, political and social vision, the design of wallpaper in Britain soon became linked with the idea of architectural control. A house designed for example by an idiosyncratic Arts and Crafts architect could not conceivably be papered in anything other than a design chosen by the architect himself.

Pugin's legacy thus took the form of the profound schism in Britain and to some extent elsewhere in northern Europe between decoration as practised by architects, and the work of interior designers working directly for clients. In France, in southern Europe, even in the United States, an interior designer is a member of a distinct profession, and can use any wallpaper they please in a new house; in Britain the architect traditionally controls the entire decorative process in a new house, and a 'decorator' rarely sets foot inside. When architectural fashion moved away from ornamentation, the idea of a well-known architect using any kind of decorative papers in a house became almost inconceivable because of the Puginesque conflict between the general architectural concept and the details of design. A look at any thorough survey of the great houses of the twentieth century—such as Richard Weston's *The House in the Twentieth Century*—will show that absolutely none of them have any decorative paper wall finishes at all.[10] Bauhaus designers tried in the 1920s to come up with simple, bland designs, which stressed the primacy of the spatial characteristics of a room: yet from an aesthetic point of view one might as well have a painted wall, especially since an increased range of paint colours offered greater variety. The eventual revival of Morris designs in the 1960s was due to a greater appreciation of Victorian architecture;

no one seems to have considered using them in a new house. The fact that many designers today see their papers as pieces of art rather than as a component of a domestic interior is nothing less than a reverberation of Pugin's view of the central role of the artist-architect.

## Wallpaper Revolutionaries 2: Laura Ashley

If Pugin's legacy was one of control, Laura Ashley, the second of the two revolutionaries, was concerned with release: in effect, she freed interior design from the control of contemporary architectural fashion, and projected a dreamy image of the imagined pleasures of the immediately pre-Pugin Regency and late Georgian eras.

At the time when Ashley established her fabric business, in an attic in Pimlico during the early 1950s, wallpaper was undergoing a minor revival after a long period of abandon by fashionable designers. In 1920s and 30s Britain, in the fashionable painted rooms of Basil Ionides and the all-white interiors of Sybil Maugham, there is almost none to be seen; Ionides' *Colour and Interior Decoration* of 1926 illustrates only extremely ornamental papers for special effects, and very few of those.[11] The overwhelming majority of designs sold at the time were pasty and artless, and beneath the consideration of fashionable interior decorators and architects.

The 1951 Festival of Britain, however, seems to have inspired the first memorable new designs for wallpapers in decades; it also marked the point at which the state-supported Council of Industrial Design began to sponsor new designers. At the art end of the market, the young Lucienne Day, alongside others like Jacqueline Groag, produced bold designs that complemented their fabrics. Their papers were designed for the London firm of John Line & Sons, who also printed designs by John Minton and other artists who were distinguished beyond the field of the applied arts. At the same time, Sanderson maintained a strong range of geometrical patterns and 'Regency' stripes. Lesley Jackson makes the point that the new strong colours may have been inspired by the current fashion in Modernist architecture for strongly painted walls.[12] Combinations of clashing patterns are illustrated in an article called "Wallpaper Revival" by Roger Smithells, in the *Daily Mail Ideal Home Book* of 1951–1952, demonstrating a fashion, thought to have come from Scandinavia, of the contrasting 'feature wall'.[13] It is however noticeable that the houses illustrated in the *Ideal Home Books* that were designed by those who were, or who became, well-known architects did not use wallpaper. Modernist architects might have used Robin Day furnishings, but they were unlikely to use Lucienne Day papers. In fact the Days themselves scarcely had any Lucienne Day paper in their own home.[14]

The *Ideal Home Books* promoted the possibility of the homeowners themselves transforming a tired house with paints and papers: together with the high quality home

journalism of the period they indicate the extent to which do-it-yourself design work was supplanting the traditional reliance on upholsterers and furnishers as exclusive purveyors of designed interiors for traditional houses. But the festival style proved to have short-lived influence in applied design, falling victim very rapidly in fashionable circles to the vicious criticism employed by Reyner Banham and the circles centred around the London art and architecture schools.[15] There was a notable falling off of interest in the subject in the *Ideal Home Books* in the years following Smithells' article. The introduction from 1961 by ICI of Vymura was an attempt to generate a new market where there was none; and in keeping with the style of the era, and presumably attempting to catch an increasing sector of young home owners, the patterns were vibrant and bold as well as shiny and dirt resistant.

Laura Ashley seems to have watched these developments with horror: she disliked modern life in general, and she was particularly repelled by the plastic, artificial nature of much contemporary design; in particular she considered vinyl papers to be "anathema".[16] Born near Merthyr Tydfil in South Wales in 1925 and trained at a secretarial college, she was not herself a designer and indeed in her early days as a fabric printer she constructed patterns made up from simple geometrical shapes, such as her long-lived *Scottish Thistle* and *Nutmeg* designs, which were composed of tiny triangles, diamonds, dots and lines. Ironically, in view of her dislike of current trends, she personally profited from the late 1960s interest in rural and folk-inspired fashion; her biographer records that the peasant-inspired dresses she was then designing were *de rigueur* at smart parties by 1970.[17] When her husband revived an idea of making papers by 1973, she entered into it with characteristic vigour. Their first papers simply adapted some of the earliest designs for fabrics, but by the end of the decade the Laura Ashley company had already established a range that had no equal for coherence and identity in British decorating.

The enduring strength of Laura Ashley as a designer is twofold: on the one hand, she relied on her own personal sense of what would be attractive; on the other, she produced ranges and catalogues that encouraged the easy creation of an entire look. Authentic Regency designs were not hard to come across by the mid-1970s. In addition to the collections of the museums, there were now a number of books, such as John Fowler and John Cornforth's renowned *English Decoration in the 18th Century* of 1974, which illustrated period interiors in detail; and many contemporary watercolours by amateur artists that gave a convincing picture of early nineteenth-century domestic life had been discovered and published.[18] The contrast between the way of life depicted in these historical records and the modern consumer market of the last gasp of the Modernist monopoly on high culture was as astounding as any that Pugin could have satirised. Contemporary editions of *House & Garden* show that the consumer had little choice beyond extremely expensive reproductions of elderly designs, and the bullying and

## PROVENCAL HALL

The warm southern sun of Provence casts deep shadows on the terracotta tiles and flagstones of farmhouse and château. Inside all is cool tranquility.
A delicate print of wild flowers in warm reds, blues and yellows can fill a room with colour and light. The soft background tone of golden ochre gently blends with the quiet yellows, greys and browns which give this region its unique feeling of rustic charm.
A tiny red diamond design on a beige ground completes this picture of simple French provincial style, which demonstrates perfectly how to use formal prints in an informal setting without appearing at all affected.

38

## DRAWING ROOM, GEORGIAN HOUSE

Provencal style hall, from *The Laura Ashley Book of Home Decorating*, 1982, p. 38.

Georgian style drawing room, from *The Laura Ashley Book of Home Decorating*, 1982, p. 40.

gaudy plastic papers of Vymura and its imitators. Sanderson's coordinated *Triad* range and its promotion of celebrities with brightly coloured papers had been a commercial success for some years, but by the mid-1970s even Sanderson's themselves seemed to have tired of promoting it.

So Ashley had a clear and appealing sense of a domestic interior that she wanted to imitate; but her success was equally due to the effective way in which she marketed her products. Customers would see how simple it was to produce the required overall effect—and thereby, of course, buy yet more of the products. In 1982 a book came out entitled *The Laura Ashley Book of Home Decorating*, by Elizabeth Dickson and Margaret Colvin, and while it was a bestseller Ashley herself disapproved of its practical approach.[19] The genius of her aesthetic was revealed to a large extent in the catalogues themselves, which illustrated faultlessly decorated but easily imitable rooms in real houses, and in a couple of special books called *Laura Ashley Decorates an English House in the Cotswolds* 1983 and *Laura Ashley Decorates a London House* 1985, which matched the catalogues in design and format, but concentrated on an entire house.[20] With engaging subtlety, there was only passing reference to the actual products used in the books, and certainly nothing so vulgar as an order reference number. It was a very clever way of raising the status of interior decoration; it also enhanced the way a resident could be personally engaged in the details of their house, in a manner that seems very fitting for the homeowner boom of the 1980s.

Laura Ashley Limited was valued on its flotation shortly after Ashley's premature death in 1985 at £270 million; her huge commercial success clearly indicates that she was offering a product for which there was tremendous demand. The Ashley range included a growing number of domestic accessories; but its success would not have been possible without wallpaper, because the most prominent surface of any domestic room is likely to be the walls. Her papers were in a sense unarchitectural: they were not intended to be subordinate to the proportions of a room; rather, they were meant to turn a room into a kind of stage set for an idealised way of life. What she had offered was a welcome relief from the didactic world of architect-oriented design that had become alternately screechy or dreary. The first edition of what became *The World of Interiors*, in November 1981, had carried no advertisements for wallpaper at all, and amongst its varied articles featured only one contemporary print; by 1987 the magazine was regularly promoting floral papers in editorial features.[21] Ashley's revolution had taken effect.

Modern designers, you will find, will aim at either a Puginian effect or an Ashley one, although they are very unlikely to admit it. The special quality of wallpaper is that it can change as you do; the world it shows is the one that you have chosen for a particular decade, or even a season. A look at designs by new entrants into the field will have a great deal to say about the kind of world we want to find behind our front doors.

1  Thummler, Sabine and Mark Turner, "Unsteady Progress: from the Turn of the Century to the Second World War", in Lesley Hoskins ed., *The Papered Wall*, London: Thames and Hudson, 1994, pp. 192–193.

2  See Nouvel-Kammer, Odile, "Wide Horizons: French Scenic Papers", in Hoskins, *The Papered Wall*, p. 110.

3  Banham, Joanna "The English Response: Mechanisation and Design Reform", in Hoskins, *The Papered Wall*, p. 136.

4  Pugin, AWN, *The True Principles of Pointed or Christian Architecture*, London: John Weale, 1841, p. 1.

5  Pugin, *The True Principles of Pointed or Christian Architecture*, p. 25.

6  Pugin's papers are described in detail in Banham, Joanna "Wallpapers", in Paul Atterbury and Clive Wainwright eds., *Pugin: a Gothic Passion*, New Haven and London: Yale University Press in association with The Victoria and Albert Museum, 1994, pp. 119–126.

7  Lloyd Wright, Frank, *An Autobiography*, first published 1932; London: Quartet Books 1977, p. 113. See also the preface by Iain Zaczek to an edition of *The Grammar of Ornament*, London: Dorling Kindersley, 2001, p. 15.

8  For an illustrated description of Morris' work as a wallpaper designer, see Hoskins, Lesley "Wallpaper", in Linda Parry ed, *William Morris*, London: Philip Wilson Publishers in association with The Victoria and Albert Museum, 1996, pp. 198–223. From 1965 Sanderson & Co, who had eventually inherited the blocks, started remaking the papers.

9  Hoskins, "Wallpaper", p. 204.

10  London: Laurence King, 2002. One house in the Modernist canon not illustrated by Weston, Patrick Gwynne's Homewood near Esher of 1937, does have a folding screen wall decorated with a Chinese paper, but this is perhaps more of a piece of furniture than a wall.

11  London: *Country Life*.

12  Jackson, Lesley *'Contemporary': Architecture and Interiors of the 1950s*, London: Phaidon, 1994, pp. 115–117.

13  Sherman, Margaret ed., *Daily Mail Ideal Home Book 1951–2*, London: Associated Newspapers Ltd, 1951, pp. 82–87.

14  The house is illustrated in Robin Day, "At the Robin Days", in Frances Lake ed., *Daily Mail Ideal Home Book 1953–4*, London: Associated Newspapers Ltd, 1953, pp. 34–39. The Days had one wall papered in a Lucienne Day design, but the article illustrates only a panel decorated with an enlargement of a Saul Steinberg drawing. Steinberg himself designed wallpapers for American manufacturers.

15  Banham was still raving against the Festival 25 years later; see Reyner Banham, "The Style: Flimsy…Effeminate", in Mary Banham and Bevis Hillier eds., *A Tonic to the Nation*, London: Thames and Hudson, 1976, pp. 190–198.

16  Sebba, Anne, *Laura Ashley: a Life by Design*, London: Weidenfeld & Nicolson, 1990, pp. 66–67; 135. I am indebted to Caroline MacDonald, who worked for Laura Ashley Ltd in the 1980s, for her comments on this section.

17  Sebba, *Laura Ashley: a Life by Design*, p. 92.

18  *London etc.*, Barrie & Jenkins. The book was republished in 1986, by which time there were several similar books available. During this period John Fowler was able to apply his schemes to several historic buildings in the care of the National Trust.

19  *The Laura Ashley Book of Home Decorating*, London: Octopus, 1982; Sebba, *Laura Ashley: a Life by Design*, p. 168.

20  The accompanying texts for both books were by Jane Clifford, and the photography by Arabella Campbell McNair-Wilson.

21  In April 1987 the magazine launched a regular feature called "Swatch", which promoted Ashley and Ashleyesque designs in large quantities. The paper featured in the first number of the magazine (which was known as *Interiors* until the edition of December 1982) was a small floral pattern by Designers Guild, to some extent similar to the type that Ashley was then reviving, pp. 68–69.

# The New Wallpaper
## Jane Audas

Wallpaper today — be it flock or photograph, mural or sticker, paper or digital screen—defies any attempt at categorisation. Designers have entered a new phase of creativity, experimenting with many different styles, applications and materials. And people are buying these papers—demonstrating a confidence to design their own interiors and a willingness to expose their taste in an overt manner. Why now though? Not since the 1950s has wallpaper been as much in the press and the public's consciousness. How has it won a new audience and renewed consideration in interior design? Wallpaper serves no practical purpose, beyond disguising uneven surfaces or cracked walls. It is an indulgence, relatively expensive and difficult to put up. Why has wallpaper resurfaced again? What needs is it fulfilling for the twenty-first century consumer?

### Doing It Yourself

In order to find out why wallpaper has come back, it is necessary to investigate wider cultures of consumption and how they have affected its revival. An availability of new styles did not cause an upturn of interest in wallpaper and in the mid-1990s it was still languishing in a back cupboard. However, the stage for its resurgence was being set. Home ownership was aided by a deregulation of credit, which allowed more people on lower incomes to secure mortgages. The consequent interest in 'Do It Yourself' home decoration sped up the cycle of decoration of homes. At one time a wall might have been papered and left for decades, but alongside these social developments constant redecoration became the norm. The decoration frenzy was fuelled by a rise in the number of television programmes and magazines about interior design. Supporting the housing boom, the media gave people the confidence to design and undertake their own DIY. This in turn was serviced by a spread of global superstores like IKEA.

In Britain, television took interior design to a mass audience, articulating ideas and providing a visual language for the nations' homes. One of the first of these programmes, *Changing Rooms*, began in 1996 and launched the profession of interior designer to the British public at large. The frenzied programme format set itself to make-over an interior against the clock. Principled on achievable design for the masses, its message was that you could change your life by changing your wallpaper. Although *Changing Rooms* was never a 'cool' programme, it drew audiences beyond its projected demographic and was quickly moved from BBC2 to BBC1 prime time. The show filled a gap in programming; people were hungry for ideas about interior decoration. The voyeuristic opportunity to see inside other people's homes and watch them decorate, or have decoration thrust upon them, was too good to miss. The point of the programme was ultimately that the viewer would feel they could and would have chosen better. Later, in 1999, with Channel 4's *Grand Designs*, the serious end

Wallpaper designed by Orla Kiely for Habitat's *VIP* collection, manufactured by Cole & Son, 2006.

Lawrence Llewelyn-Bowen, presenter of cult television show, *Changing Rooms*. © Llewelyn-Bowen Ltd. www.llb.co.uk

Front cover of *Wallpaper\**, April 2005. Picture supplied courtesy of Wallpaper\*, IPC Media. © Phillip Toledano www.ptoledano.com

Front cover of the IKEA 2007 catalogue.

of the viewing spectrum was addressed. The programme showed ambitious self-build projects and its presenter Kevin McCloud articulated good design to an avid, design-savvy audience. It was more about construction than decoration but its popularity as a programme clearly demonstrated the passion that homes evoked in the British public. It eventually spawned its own magazine in 2004 and a live show in 2006.

## On the Shelf

Accompanying the television coverage, a flurry of new magazine titles were launched in the late 1990s and early 2000s, cashing in on this wave of interest in interiors. Soon there were more than 20 titles available. Month after month they contained articles about new furniture, aspirational photographic spreads on perfectly styled homes, and page after page of ideas for redecorating. At the bottom end of the market were magazines like *Your Home* and *Perfect Home*. They contained articles on the way to achieve looks similar to the homes featured and shopping ideas from the high street. At the other end of the market titles like *Wallpaper\** and *World of Interiors* did not envisage their readers actually doing their own DIY but featured international interiors styled 'just so' and new or vintage designer furniture, placed like museum exhibits. Between these types of magazine were titles like *Elle Decoration* and *Living Etc.*, publications that the new urban homeowners with an interest in design would read. For such label-conscious readers the name behind the design was important. But they could as easily be persuaded of the merits of small, one off craft-produced wallpaper as a mass-produced one from an interiors shop like Habitat.

So, if the public were now brimming with ideas how were they to realise them? The expanding motorway-visible, hangar-like DIY shops became regular weekend destinations, queues at checkouts notwithstanding. In order to facilitate the new homeowners' latent interior design talents, many of these shops had begun to offer room settings and a plethora of colour-coordination hints. Products were grouped together and photographs hung so that it was possible to see what your rooms might look like when finished. Not a lot was left to the imagination. The main contender in the interior decoration market was IKEA, the Swedish manufacturer that opened its first store in the US in 1985 and in the UK in 1987. IKEA cleverly expanded interest through a catalogue, which was posted free to specially targeted areas. IKEA was (and is) an enabler, making it very easy for people to get bright modern design cheaply and instantly. High street chain stores also began to expand into interiors or to expand existing ranges. They saw the potentially lucrative market that was opening up and offered rejuvenated interiors ranges, often designed by 'named' designers. Interior design was trading under a global aesthetic. The upper end of the market flourished too, with fashion designers moving in, putting the designer label on products very similar to those sold in the cheaper superstores. The ultimate irony of labelling happened when the designer Ralph Lauren repackaged the quintessential British look and sold it not just to his fellow Americans, but back to the British as well.

## Chuck Out Your Chintz

Interior design was now demystified and democratised, easily available at the high and low ends of the market, setting the scene for wallpaper's revival, the icing on the cake of an interior design scheme. But this revival was slow in coming, lagging behind other interior decorations such as paint, textiles, lighting and furniture. IKEA didn't manufacture wallpaper and few of the other shops showed much interest in it. They usually stocked the blandest, safest designs—or plain lining papers to take advantage of the burgeoning paint market—nothing to offend. Of course wallpaper continued to be manufactured, sold and used throughout but its 'time' had yet to come. Years of woodchip and nasty, slightly shiny, pastel flowered wallpapers had scarred the public's collective memory. Though people could easily identify the vintage of a wallpaper uncovered whilst decorating—be it the orange and sticky brown papers of the 1970s or the faded patterns of the 1930s—they had no notion of what a truly modern wallpaper could look like.

There was also a pressure on people not to give in too much to patterned decoration, spearheaded by IKEA's advertising campaign exhorting everyone to 'chuck out your chintz'. Along with the boom in home-ownership came the need to protect that investment. As soon as the initial wave of interest in decorating a first home had passed, there came television programmes and magazines on how to sell and move on up the property ladder. The very ephemerality of wallpaper worked against it. It was seen as an expensive investment that couldn't be taken with you when you move. People became scared of making individualistic statements with their interior designs that would make the property potentially unsellable. Homeowners were warned not to inject too much personality into their homes, to give prospective new owners a 'blank canvas' onto which to project their own dreams and decorations. The age of beige was ushered in.

As the housing market in Britain slowed down by the early twenty-first century the constant pressure to maintain show-home standards relaxed. Personality in decoration began to appear around the house again and all that tasteful minimalism had piles of clutter stacked up on top of it. However strong the advice to keep walls plain and furnishings to a minimum had been, the British love of eccentricity reared its colourful head once again, and wallpaper provided the perfect backdrop.

Minimal interior, from the *Tylösand* range by IKEA.

Wallpaper designed by Eley Kishimoto for Habitat, manufactured by Cole & Son.

Wallpaper designed by Matthew Williamson for Habitat, manufactured by Cole & Son.

Though it was slow in coming, the revival is gathering pace. High street shops have begun to show an interest in this revival. Habitat has just launched a small range of designer-celebrity wallpapers under their *Very Important Product* (VIP) range. Commissioned from fashion and product designers including Matthew Williamson and Orla Kiely, the designs are tastefully safe, aimed at a mass market that is still making up its mind about pattern.

But the signs are good and wherever you look—on the internet, in small quirky boutique shops and generic high street chains—there are exciting, innovative and life-enhancing wallpapers out there.

## The Designs

The correlations between art and applied design are, during any period, undeniable. This is true for wallpaper as much as any other form of design. The fine arts both reflect and are influenced by the visual cultures surrounding them. As a plethora of visual material—advertising, window displays, film and theatre sets, fashion and interiors—came to the fore with the rise of mass markets and mass-production from the late nineteenth century onwards, they began to provide subject matter for fine artists, who began to work seriously with applied design. The final work would not be as valued commercially or aesthetically as their fine art output but it would touch more directly on people's lives. The role of the commercial artist evolved, working to commission in many different areas including wallpaper design. By the 1930s, artist-designed textiles and wallpapers were often featured in advertisements, raising awareness of particular brands. But today, when artists' stories are told in books and exhibited in galleries, very often this commercial work is left out because of its association with mass-production. It was been left to museums, committed to showcasing product and industrial design, to exhibit the missing pieces of the story. Unlike the other graphic arts, however, wallpaper was little exhibited or collected even by museums, with the exception of the Victoria and Albert Museum (V&A), the Geffrye Museum and MODA in London and the Whitworth Art Gallery, Manchester. While a few books contain historical surveys of wallpaper, they give little room to contemporary wallpaper, resulting in the relative obscurity of many wallpaper designers.

Yet artists, designers, architects and craftspeople continue to be drawn to wallpaper as a medium for creative expression. There is a permanence about it that is attractive to designers, but it is also an artistic medium that directly affects people's lives. Sometimes these wallpapers are for mass production; very often they are small batch productions by small design agencies or individuals. Their papers provide a backdrop to everyday domestic life or enliven a commercial space. As the story of contemporary wallpaper is increasingly articulated and the availability of the wallpapers themselves becomes more widespread, the consumer becomes increasingly aware of the many decorative possibilities before them. The knowing consumer continues to move ahead, looking for other ways to individualise their space. And so the market hots up. The designers in this book are one step ahead of the game, and their work is leading the way to an ever more innovative wallpaper.

The aesthetic delineation between designs for urban and provincial interiors is less marked today than it has ever been. Availability of good mass-market design has smoothed out many distinctions and traditions. Kitsch designs once deemed suitable only for the mass-market have been re-appropriated and repackaged for the sophisticated urban consumer. Designers draw upon all kinds of historic wallpaper styles, twisting together a myriad of influences to make a contemporary genre. The people who buy these wallpapers, too, are less concerned about 'what people might think' and are more willing to experiment, reserving the right to play with their interiors, to use a floral pattern in a city bedroom or to bring a vivid, large scaled abstract wallpaper into a small living room. Yet it is precisely because we associate certain wallpaper designs with certain historical periods that these papers can now inject irony and humour into a postmodern interior. Wallpaper now provides backdrops to iconic furniture—perhaps covering only one wall, enough but not too much pattern. It also gives instant vintage credibility to a room full of antique pieces. The very fact that not everyone uses wallpaper today makes its statement that much more compelling.

Taking an overview of contemporary wallpaper it soon becomes clear that there are strong, stylistic themes influencing designers today. However, even though individual wallpapers can be grouped under different sections of a book, many of the designers are making wallpapers in several different styles and what defines their work is the designer's distinctive authorship and own individuality of approach. The different chapters of this volume: Decorative, Figurative, Abstract, Architectrural and Interactive, therefore represent broad stroke movements in wallpaper today, and each designer featured is recognised for breaking new ground in design innovation within the field.

## The Future

What is next for wallpaper? Can the creative boundaries be pushed further? The word itself has been re-appropriated for computers, referring to the digital images that people choose to use as a backdrop for their computer screens. Googling the word wallpaper calls up more pages for desktop wallpapers than paper ones. Often one of the first things people do when they get a new computer, or are assigned one at work, is to choose their own 'wallpaper' for it. The use of the word in this context is imparting a domestic cosiness to technology.

*Rooted in Time and Motion*, garden shed installation with cress and mustard seed, grass and inbuilt irrigation system at *The Other Flower Show*, the Victoria and Albert Museum, 2004, by Heather Barnett.

*Moving Wallpaper*, paper
and conductive ink, 2002,
by Simon Heijdens.

Designers, particularly young graduates who are still unfettered by commercial constraints, are also utilising new technologies for a new generation of interactive wallpapers. Dutch designer Simon Heijdens, who studied at the Design Academy Eindhoven, produced a moving wallpaper for his graduation project in 2002. Printed with temperature-reacting Thermochrome Inks, the patterns of the wallpaper alter, disappear and reappear. In a further step, Christopher Pearson produced digitally animated wallpaper for his Royal College of Art graduation project, which has now developed into a series entitled *Look at Your Walls.* These are solely intended for viewing on a screen. The first of these wallpapers used William Morris's seminal Victorian design: *Willow Boughs.* A leafy delicate pattern, Pearson digitally animated it so that it moves and alters in subtle ways, as though the breeze is blowing through the leaves, playing with our assumptions and expectations.

As large plasma screen televisions and home projection systems are now more widespread in homes, these digital wallpapers begin to have obvious applications. Somewhere between a desktop wallpaper and real wallpaper, projecting a wallpaper onto a wall, having it alter, move or change daily is a distinct possibility. Indeed, British digital artist Daniel Brown's screen-based animated flowers are now in several private homes and ritzy hotels. This development allows you to take your wallpaper with you when you move. Truly wallpapers for a restless generation.

But, wallpaper—the real thing—is once again on a design high. Paper has tactile and ephemeral qualities that continue to be valued and to give value to interiors. Wallpaper has an intimate connection with the home and its inhabitants, it says so much more about the person who lives in a space than painted walls, however colourful. It reveals tastes and makes one vulnerable to the opinions of others. Yet, at the same time wallpaper cocoons and covers an interior, repaying the investment required through personal expression. It is the hope of this book to broaden the scope of contemporary wallpaper's audience, both to students and academics who may design and study wallpapers, but also to people looking for ideas for decorating their own homes. Let us unroll the new wallpaper.

*Willow Boughs,* 2005,
by Christopher Pearson.

*Marney's Lace Olive,*
silkscreen, 2002,
by Louise Body.

Decorative

There is a comfort in a contemporary design that is reminiscent, yet different, to an historic one. It gives all sorts of connotations to an interior and is a strong way to modernise a room, yet to retain a domestic scale. Decorative wallpaper has been in production and on our walls for centuries. Often utilising floral or repeat patterns, these papers were first manufactured in the eighteenth century, and versions of the flowery chintzes and small repeat patterns characteristic of this era are still popular today. The naturalistic floral papers from Arts and Crafts designer William Morris fall into this category and the quintessential Laura Ashley wallpapers, with their neo-Georgian repeats, kept this style alive throughout the latter quarter of the twentieth century. Cole & Son has literally kept this tradition alive, using the same prints and techniques that were in vogue in Victorian times. Linda Florence has revived the concept of damask wallpaper, but given it a modern spin, with her use of silvery 'scratchcard' material that can hide or expose the traditional pattern underneath.

The flowering wallpaper has also received a more modern overhaul. Jane Gordon Clark's Ornamenta company based in London, whose productions are very much in the Chelsea interiors style, also produces a site-specific paper range titled *Hot House Flowers*. These oversized, super-real, exotic flower designs have often been reproduced in interiors magazines looking to highlight new interpretations of this most traditional style. In many ways it is simply the sheer scale of the design that makes them appear modern, though they retain a certain softness. This dramatic retelling of the floral wallpaper has been made possible by advances in reprographic techniques, which have influenced many different styles of wallpapers, but few so dramatically as the floral genre.

Although decorative wallpaper is traditionally seen as an unassuming (even safe) choice for decorating, it remains multidimensional in purpose and effect. The chintzes and florals are seen as a feminine genre of wallpaper as their designs often parallel or mimic textile designs associated with dress fabrics. But the denser, darker, Victorian-style decorative wallpapers, designed to give weight and grandeur to a room are more masculine in effect, with the boldest of this style being the flocked papers, which were originally based on eighteenth century silk damask fabrics. Coming down off an initial high perch, they were often used in pubs and cheap hotels during the 1970s and 1980s when they were produced with lighter colour combinations, often gold and red, or gold and green. The flock wallpaper has recently been re-appropriated by high-end boutique clubs and retail spaces, where the paper can cleverly carried off if used ironically. It is the subconscious recognition of a style that draws us to these patterns, but it is the designer's eye that has re-drawn them for a new audience.

# Louise Body

Louise Body's designs are playfully nostalgic but decidedly contemporary. Using a process of hand-printing and hand-finishing, rooted in wallpaper tradtion Body has updated the classic floral patterned wallpaper for the postmodern homeowner. Her pressed flower patterns are simple and elegant silhouettes in earthy, warm tones, which are eye-catching and graphic, recalling Warhol's work, but measured in their use of colour. These bold graphic elements are often paired with subtle, lacy patterns and highly tactile surfaces. Her more recent bird themed prints are reminiscent of nature magazine illustrations, which dissolve into pattern through their serial repetition. Body's work has many touchstones: Arts and Crafts patterns, 1960s Pop Art, and 70s colour schemes.

Designs like *Birds and Lace* and *Flowerpress* use a layering technique, taking a base of lace, or fern leaves, and printing over them with clear figurative drawings of birds in cages, or silhouettes of flowers. In *Garden Birds* and *Birdies*, similar themes are explored, but in a more focussed space, creating a sense of movement and fluidity.

Body's company has been in business since 2003 when she received a grant from the Prince's Trust. All of her pieces are printed using water-based inks and she avoids using any hazardous solvents in the printing process. In addition, her paper comes from managed forests and any paper waste is recycled. In this way her 'slow-design' approach allows her to maintain a progressive, sustainable process.

1

1  *Garden Birds*, silkscreen and hand-finished, 2001.
2  *Birdies*, silkscreen and hand-finished, 2003
3  *Autumn Woods*, silkscreen, 2001.
4  *Bird and Lace*, silkscreen and hand-finished, 2003.
5  *Marneys Lace Charcoal*, silkscreen, 2002.
6  *Flowerpress*, silkscreen, 2001.
7  *Harry's Garden*, silkscreen and hand-finished, 2002.
8  *Pavillion Birds*, hand-finished flexoprint, 2004.

2

3

4

5

6

7

8

# Manuel Canovas

Using modern technology and a modern sensibility, Manuel Canovas makes faithful reproductions of classic *toile-de-jouy* fabric prints. *Toile-de-jouy* refers to the eighteenth century method of fabric printing using engraved copper plates. This huge leap in technology allowed textile designers to reproduce highly detailed images accurately and cheaply. French craftsmen appropriated images from famous paintings and contemporary prints, introducing an element of narrative into the otherwise static world of textiles.

Continuing in this very prestigious and very French tradition, Canovas has adapted the distinctive look of *toile-de-jouy* fabrics for paper wall coverings. He uses similar motifs such as romantic gardens, flirting lovers and rural idlers as well as oriental and exotic themes, often culled from actual eighteenth century French art of the same vintage. What separates his designs from the *toile* originals is his daring use of colour, a far cry from the conservative and naturalistic palette of Rococo France. His vibrant tones dominate but don't overpower the rooms they fill. Combinations like a pink engraving on an army green background or grey flowers over tomato red make the subtle engravings dynamic and modern.

As well as these clear references, his work is also informed by his interest in Japanese design, American folk art and even a curiosity in botany. In business since 1963, the Manuel Canovas fabric house has applied these designs to not just walls but textiles, pillows, chairs and even swimwear. Whatever the format, a Canovas pattern is instantly recognisable and his penchant for tasteful and sophisticated images and vivid colour has made him an international success.

1

2

3

4

1 *Papiers Peints* Volume 1, 2006.
2 *Papiers Peints* Volume 1, 2006.
3 *Nantes*, rose, 2006.
4 *Pali*, moka, 2006.

## Cole & Son

Cole & Son is one of the oldest and most distinguished printing houses in the wallpaper industry. Dating back to 1873, this prestigious company has adorned the walls of the Palace of Westminster, the Brighton Pavilion, Buckingham Palace and even the White House. Many contemporary designers have developed new and exciting motifs for the company, but much of Cole & Son's inspiration comes from their own illustrious back catalogue. All their designs are executed using much the same techniques they employed when the company was founded.

Block printing is the oldest of these techniques and is a painstaking process, which requires highly skilled printers and allows no room for error. It utilises a thick ink, which gives their papers an almost relief-like quality. Their archive boasts over 1,800 block designs from past and present. The majority of their designs utilise the surface printing technique in which ink is applied with a roller by a very steady hand. The final printing method is screen-printing. Cole & Son set up one of very first screen-printing studios in the late 1940s. Screen-printing produces highly detailed patterns by forcing ink through a blocked off design in thin silk or gauze. Flocking, which simulates velvet by applying glue and wool particles, was rediscovered by Cole & Son owner John Perry in the 1870s.

It is perhaps the postmodernist revival of once outmoded forms, which has made Cole & Son more popular than ever. Now these prestigious wall coverings find homes on the walls of stately homes as well as urban design conscious apartments. And with tailor-made colours and patterns anyone can have wallpaper that is both original and authentic.

1  *Butterflies and Dragonflies*, screen print, 1950–1960s.
2  *Optimum Woods*, screen print, 1950–1960s.
3  *Malabar*, screen print, 1950–1960s.
4  *Paradise Tree*, 1920s.

1

2

3

4

# Neisha Crosland

Neisha Crosland is something of a polymath. Her design range encompasses clothing, fabric furnishing, underwear, and of course, wallpaper, and her popularity has skyrocketed in recent years. Her delicate floral designs have a hand-drawn feel to them, which conveys a warmth and an individuality to a room. The prints are hand-painted on silk, with a luxury finish, and all this has made them increasingly desirable.

The influences on Crosland's designs are varied. *Clematis* indicates an awareness of the Chinoiserie tradition. The spaced patterning and fluid curves of the stems are reminiscent of the brush-strokes of traditional Oriental art. *Caravan* is an intelligent interpretation of 1970s design, specifically that found in mobile homes of the period. In all her prints, the use of colour is carefully considered. Unlikely combinations such as blue and orange or pink and green are so delicately treated, that they manage to be simultaneously pleasing and eye-catching. The muted motifs are brought to life with white highlights and a careful balance of strength and softness. The relative proportions between the shapes and the way that they sit on the background indicates the touch of a master.

Crosland's portfolio has reached the mainstream with her *Romagna* collection, developed with Osbourne and Little, however her independent range, which is kept under her own name, remains resolutely exclusive.

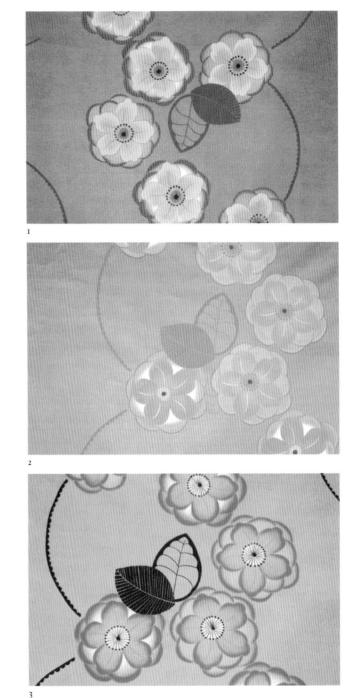

1

2

3

1 *Clematis* in copper, from the *Silk Wallpaper* range, digital print, 2005.
2 *Clematis* in olive.
3 *Clematis* in pink.
4 *Berryflower* in Marrakesh blue, digital print, 2005.
5 *Cactus Paisley* in Marrakesh blue, digital print, 2005.
6 *Caravan* in chocolate, digital print, 2005.

4

5

6

# Linda Florence

Central St Martins graduate Linda Florence's innovative wallpaper designs have proved a great hit with collectors and high end companies. Using gold leaf, leather and other exotic materials, her wallpaper has a tactile quality to it that speaks of luxury and also questions the way we perceive luxury. Her *Morphic Damask* wallpaper series borrows the bold tones and luxurious materials of eastern textiles but mixes the traditional with computer-generated patterns and 80s day-glo colours.

Forming part of her *Scratchcard* series *Modern Damask* modern interpretation of damask, substituting what would have been hand-woven sections of gold and silver thread with the silvery foil material of Lottery scratchcards. The home-owner can scratch off the foil to reveal the colours of the design underneath—or can leave it partially unscratched to create a mottled effect. The child-like anticipation that everyone experiences when finding out whether they've won is rewarded every single time. The prize becomes not what's underneath, but the anticipation and excitement itself.

The layering of patterns and colours in Florence's designs give her traditional designs a spatial depth that challenges the viewer and demands closer examination and engagement.

Details of *Morphic Damask* from the *Scratchcard* collection, 2005.

# Fromental

Fromental's hand-made, bespoke wallpapers are designed to the precise specifications of the walls they are intended to cover. Printing on both paper and silk, the distinctive prints are panoramic and non-repeating. They have 16 ranges, each finding their inspiration in different sources; 1930s florals, 1950s conversational features, and eighteenth century Chinoiserie. This latter term refers to a popular style in the 1750s and 60s, which was inspired by the porcelain, silk and lacquerware that was starting to be imported from China and Japan, and which caused a spate of emulations by English designers.

The embroidered silk collections feature hand-sewn patterns in silk thread onto a fine silk background. The launch collection was a selection of stripes, stitched in an almost infinite range of colours, with part printed, part embroidered delicate butterfly and blossom tree pattern. The Asiatic themes speak of tradition mixed with experimental flair.

Each panel takes weeks to produce by craftsmen in China, and the resulting luxury is literally tangible. An installation for private villas at the Wynn in Las Vegas required approximately 146,500 metres of silk thread and 20,000 hours of work. Although embroidery is not usually associated with contemporary design, the result of their painstaking work is a very chic product that does not vie for space, but quietly lends a room a subtle air of opulence.

Tim Butcher and Lizzie Deshayes run the company from the headquarters in West London. Butcher has his background in the renowned Chinoiserie house, de Gournay, hence the Chinese influence. "I wanted to make something that had the same fine detail and craftsmanship but was very contemporary and clean", he says. The company is very new to the market but has been very well received by design critics the world over, and has been widely publicised in decoration magazines.

1

2

1   *Variegated Leaves: Byzant*, hand-painted using emulsion on paper, 2005.
2   *Chinese Sparrows: French House*, 2005.
3   *Bamboo Moon: Chocolate*, hand-painted, 2004.
4   *Nonsuch: Jade*, hand-painted on silk, 2005.
5   *Nonsuch: Armando*, hand-painted on silk, 2005.
6   *Amelie: Alcazar*, 2005.
7   *Jardin au Bamboo: Congo*, hand-painted using emulsion on paper, 2005.
8   *Chinese Sparrows: Sunflower Silk*, hand-painted on silk, 2005.
9   *Funky Bamboo: Tropicana*, hand-painted on silk, 2005.
10  *Willow: Mardi Gras*, hand-painted using emulsion on paper, 2005.
11  *Variegated Leaves: Heather*, hand-painted using emulsion on paper, 2005.

Overleaf left:
*Paradiso: Copper Iron*, hand-painted on silk, 2005.

Overleaf right:
*Paradiso: Bubblegum Blue*, hand-painted on silk, 2005.

3

4

5

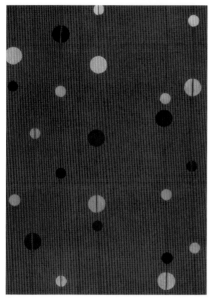

6

7

8

9

10

11

# Jane Gordon Clark

Jane Gordon Clark's work is not constrained by the muted colours and patterns of traditional wall coverings. Working under the design label Ornamenta, Clark is best known for pioneering large-scale printed wallpapers, in which digital images are applied like a mural to an entire wall. The first of this series, *Hot House Flowers* is photographs of tiny flowers printed on a monumental scale. These wall-sized images barely read as flowers, instead forming a pattern, albeit an irregular one, out of colours and shapes. This concept takes the idea of the floral motif literally—presenting the flowers themselves unaltered. The only patterns are those already present in nature.

Using more traditional design elements, the *Spatial Graphics* line features common patterns like diamonds, wavy lines or rectangles printed in metallic inks on rich toned backgrounds which gradually shift in colour from floor to ceiling. This unusal patterning technique makes her shapes jump out, occassionally creating the illusion of indents and niches in the walls as the subtly shifting tones oscillate up and down.

Aside from her digital prints, Ornamenta's papers are generally hand-printed and individually tailored to specific environments. This hand-made feel is especially evident in her *Natural Petals* line, which is made out of mulberry bark mulch to create a unique texture full of natural variations and accidents.

While her patterns have an almost austere elegance and traditional character, they are a dominant force in any room and suggest bold new possibilities for matching decoration and furnishings.

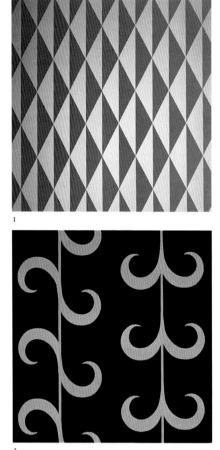

1

2

3

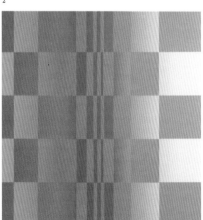

4

5

1 *Vice Versa*, hand-printed wallpaper, 2002.
2 *Arabesque*, hand-printed wallpaper, 2004.
3 *Swerve*, from the *Spatial Graphics* collection, 2004.
4 *Indent*, from the *Spatial Graphics* collection, 2004.
5 *Square Crazy*, from the *Spatial Graphics* collection, 2004.
6 *Linear Leaf*, hand-printed wallpaper, 2004.
7 *Orange Lilies*, from the *Hot House Flowers* collection, 2000.
8 *Springtime Marigold*, from the *Natural Petal* collection, 2002.
9 *Magenta Orchid Room*, from the *Hot House Flowers* collection, 2000.

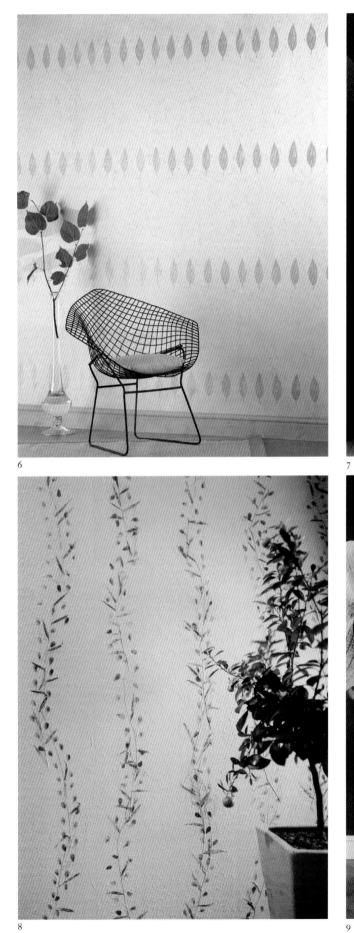

6

7

8

9

## Hemingway Design

The husband and wife duo of Wayne and Gerardine Hemingway are probably better known as the fashion label Red or Dead which dominated British fashion runways for over 20 years with their street style designs. Starting as a modest stall in Camden Market making outfits for the disco, new-wave, and new romantic scene, Red or Dead soon became a major label, and was sold off in 1999. The Hemingways have since set up a new label called Hemingway Design, which continues their mission to make good design that is accessible to everyone, and whilst their colour palette may have become tempered over the years, their rebellious attitude toward design has not.

Their *4walls* range for Graham and Brown is an example of large-scale design, which is intended to create an impact in a room. Some of the range contains intelligent and considered referencing to the designs of previous decades. *Tiffany* openly alludes to the Art Nouveau swirls and curves of the infamous jewellers. *Matchstick* indicates an inspiration by 1950s geometric patterning, and *Barking*, which is a bold emulation of inlaid wood, looks like it could have been found on the rec room walls of a house in the 1970s. By acknowledging these influences, but reinterpreting them to tally with the design sensibilities of the twenty-first century, the kitsch aspects are toned down, and with a small nod to irony, the designs take on a whole new slant, best suited to feature walls, or for large spaces.

Their other designs, such as *Hula Hoop* and *Stripe* are conceptually simple ideas embellished with careful arrangements of colour and texture, providing a context which the room can be designed around (as depicted). The wallpaper is priced to reflect Hemingways left-leaning politics. "We've got mass-market taste", says Wayne proudly, "which is why, rather than doing wallpaper for £60 a roll, we design—and use —wallpaper that costs £14.99 a roll from a DIY store."

1

2

3

5

1 *Tiffany*, from the *4walls* collection for
  Graham and Brown, 2005.
2 *Barking*, from the *4walls* collection for
  Graham and Brown, 2005.
3 *Stripe*, from the *4walls* collection for Graham
  and Brown, 2005.
4 *Hulahoop*, from the *4walls* collection for
  Graham and Brown, 2005.
5 *Matchstick*, from the *4walls* collection for
  Graham and Brown, 2005.

4

# The Magnificent Chatwin Brothers

Anselm and Sam Chatwin, a.k.a. The Magnificent Chatwin Brothers, are a London-based duo, whose distinctly individual look has proved very popular amongst the London design set.

Coming from a fashion design and a graphic design background, respectively, the brothers are clearly influenced by traditional British design; however, they also cite Rockabilly, Americana, comics and tattoos as sources of inspiration. Their *Skulls* wallpaper was based around a traditional Russian sailor tattoo. The faintly tribal death-heads are interwoven with delicate vines and hearts, which from far away looks oddly traditional, and almost Morris-like. *Swallows* also started life as a naval tattoo. The simple dark brush-strokes of the stylised swallows creates a layering effect on the bold colour backgrounds.

Both *Skulls* and *Swallows* are hand-printed wallpapers that come in a range of colours (*Skulls* even has a limited edition glow-in-the-dark version), but the brothers have a second range of less exclusive, digitally-printed papers. The most popular of these is *Lightning*. With a very different feel to *Swallows* and *Skulls*, this is a very cool contemporary, two-colour print. The lightening bolts are cleverly interleaved with one another, facing in both directions, creating a pattern that initially seems like a chaotic scribble and only reveals its geometry upon closer inspection. Printed in delicate shades of lilac and peppermint green, the result is a dynamic pattern that lends a contemporary, fun look to a room without overpowering it.

1  *Swallows*, hand silk-screen printed, 2005.
2  *Swallows*, in situ.
3  *Skulls*, hand silk-screen printed, 2005.
4  *Lightning*, flexographic printing, 2006.
5  *Skulls*, detail.

1

2

3

5

4

## Timorous Beasties

With one foot firmly planted in the tradition of William Morris and another in the edgy world of urban grit, the award winning Timorous Beasties' designs create a provocative feast of pattern and images. Their iconoclastic style is defined by uncompromisingly contemporary images intricately woven into the language of traditional print. When tramps, junkies and prostitutes are devilishly patterned into pre-revolutionary French *toile* designs, as with their *Glasgow Toile* 2004, one can't deny the dark wit behind their expert execution.

"Beasties" are a common facet of their designs, with insects and bugs often crawling or flying across the plane. Such embellishments are references to oriental influences. Their wallpaper prints consistently employ experimental concepts and colours juxtaposed with pre-modern and eastern themes. Often their carefully chosen colours serve to diffuse harsh lines and make the forms visually bleed into one another, becoming more a colour field than an articulated pattern.

Timorous Beasties design and produce their textiles and wallpapers under the same roof, maintaining the integrity of the product from design board to wall space. As designer-producers they crucially maintain control over all aspects of the pieces, allowing them to fashion wallpaper that is in every way tailored to its specific environment. Whilst rooting their identity, through motif and practice, firmly in their native Glasgow, Timorous Beasties exercise a control over their works rarely possible in this age of mass-production.

1

2

3

4

1 *Glasgow Toile*, hand-printed onto fabric, 2001.
2 *Buterfly*, hand-printed flat bed silk screen onto paper, 2004.
3 *Insects*, hand-printed flat bed silk screen onto paper, 1998.
4 *Megegan Rose*, hand-printed flat bed silk screen onto paper, 1991.
5 *English Pheasant*, hand-printed flat bed silk screen onto paper, 1997.
6 *Thistle*, hand-printed flat bed silk screen onto paper, 1997.
7 *Fresco*, hand-printed flat bed silk screen onto paper, 1998.

Overleaf left:
*Oriental Orchid*, hand-printed flat bed silk screen onto paper, 2005.

Overleaf right:
*Euro Damask*, hand-printed flat bed silk screen onto paper, 2001.

5

6

7

# Twenty2

Brooklyn based company Twenty2 skilfully straddles the wallpaper market, catering to both contemporary and more conservative tastes. Husband and wife duo Robertson and Kyra Harnett design wallpaper which is meant to work with almost any interior instead of competing with it for attention. Their designs draw on modern motifs from the 1950s, 60s and 70s which are refined, updated and stripped of their kitsch connotations.

Many ranges, like their grasscloth papers, evoke fond memories of grandparents' homes, minus the dated colour scheme. Other ranges, which might have once decorated a classic American dinner, are made more agreeable by fainter lines and softer colours. Elsewhere, retro 50s palettes are applied successfully to more contemporary designs.

Even their avant-garde leanings are tempered by their characteristic restraint. Tangential lines and subtle colours break up what could have been a stark Mondrian-like grid. Other daring patterns are closed off in tiny circles or within their favourite recurring motif of a gingko leaf. Although Twenty2's designs are highly versatile and intended to fit with a variety of decorative styles, the Harnetts understand the importance of personalised design and continue to fulfil private commissions and tailor their designs to individual settings. A far cry from some of the uncompromising and sometimes brash wallpaper experiments of their contemporaries, Twenty2 fashions practical designs for use in the average home and celebrates the quaint American vernacular style.

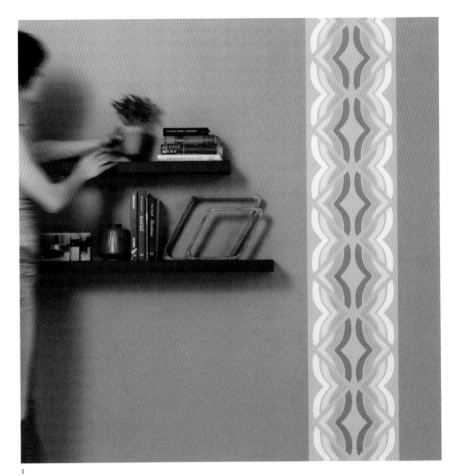

1

2

1  *Dixon* in eve gray, from the *Wallband* collection, flexographic printing on a prepasted, non-woven, washable and removable material, 2005.

2  *Montague* in shower, from the *Wallband* collection, flexographic printing on a prepasted, non-woven, washable and removable material, 2004.

3  *Maxwell* in grenadine, from the *Wallband* collection, flexographic printing on a prepasted, non-woven, washable and removable material, 2003.

4  *Casamila* in grenadine, from the *Wallband* collection, flexographic printing on a prepasted, non-woven, washable and removable material, 2003.

5  *Columbia Heights* in antifreeze, from the *Wallband* collection, flexographic printing on a prepasted, non-woven, washable and removable material, 2003.

6  *Montague Terrace* in glimmer, printed on gold mylar, 2004.

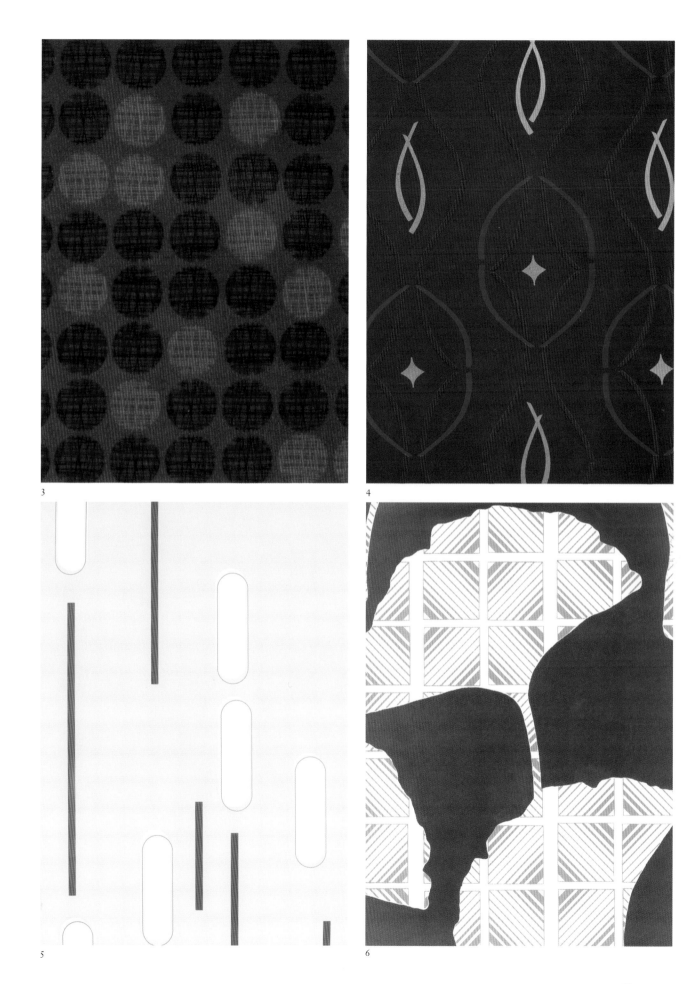

3

4

5

6

# Erica Wakerly

Erica Wakerly's background in illustration clearly shows through in her work. Her first collection has a quirky, varied and fresh feel, and plays with ideas of perspective, reflection and contrast. Her *Angles* design is a bold, geometric pattern in a sophisticated repeat, that when hung becomes subtle and ethereal, its metallic lines seeming to conduct light across the surface of the wall like a kind of geometric cobweb.

Her *Houses* design, on the other hand, has a completely different feel and effect. This is a playful yet haunting design of different types and shapes of houses, each set in their own space and separate from one another. Many of the buildings seem to lean dangerously or have a skewed perspective that gives an unbalanced, unsettling effect, creating a weird tableau of isolation, that highlights the way we demarcate our personal space.

*Spiral* again plays with the idea of perspective and creates a three-dimensional effect through a clever use of pattern. The paper can be hung either vertically or horizontally, depending on the space available, and gives two very different looks. The pattern is a geometric yet organic design that has a strong visual impact, yet is also subtle and calming. Wakerly achieves this by giving the design a strong, circular focal point that draws in the eye and creates a kind of 'eye of the storm' tranquillity that belies the geometric patterns surrounding.

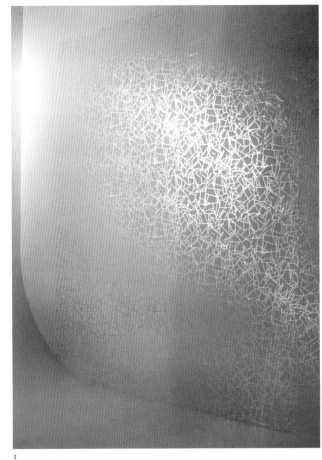

I

2

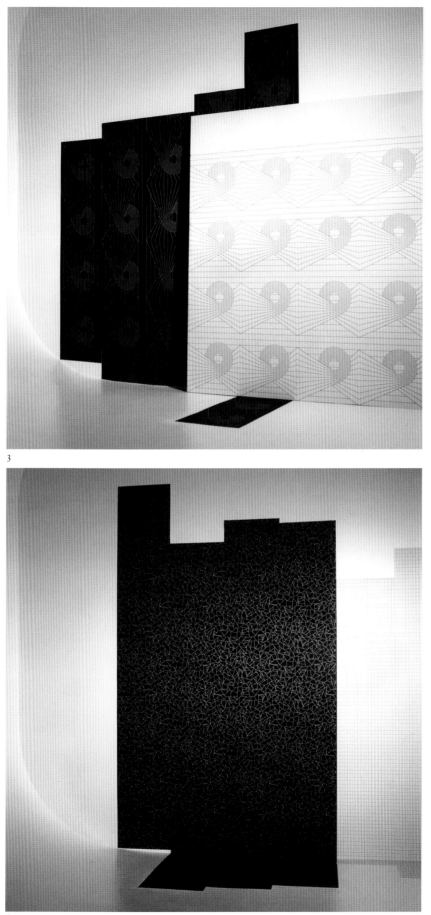

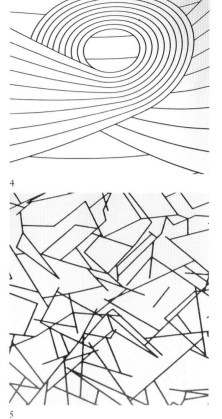

1 *Angles*, surface print on foil, 2005.
2 *Houses*, flexographic print/paper, 2006.
3 *Spiral*, flexographic print /paper, 2005.
4 *Spiral*, detail, flexographic print/paper, 2005.
5 *Angles*, surface print on foil, 2005.
6 *Windmill*, flexographic print/paper, 2006.

Figurative

The telling of stories on walls has a long history, from cave and wall paintings, through to tapestries, graffiti and the recent revival of figurative and narrative wallpapers. The early examples of this style, like the *toile-de-jouy* papers which evolved in France in the eighteenth century, contained small vignettes idealising the subject matter of everyday life or illustrating special state occasions. The use of figurative styles remained popular for children's rooms until the end of the twentieth century. A new way of visualising stories on wallpapers developed in the twenty-first century, using a new visual language drawn from comics and popular art. The term coined for this style—'superflat'—was initially coined in reference to the world as depicted in Japanese manga cartoons and animations, peculiarly two-dimensional and child-like. Designers have applied this style to wallpaper with the intention that it will resonate with a (mainly younger) generation who are familiar with this Japanese cartoon-like imagery. These wallpapers are reminiscent of illustrations being produced for films, comics, skateboards and CD covers, but they are designed on a much larger scale and with consideration for the repeat patterns needed for wallpaper.

In superflat wallpaper (and, to some extent, textiles) the stories being told are not of urban subjects as they are in the comics; the designers are making wallpapers that depict a more fantastical natural world. They are about whimsy and a child-like appreciation of story telling yet they are delivered in a very adult wallpaper. Swedish designer Hanna Werning has produced highly decorative figurative wallpapers, which have great movement and life using a limited, yet sophisticated palette with layers of colourful foliage obscuring silhouettes of roaming animals and insects. Figurative wallpapers also come in a more restrained form and on a smaller scale, such as those by British designers Absolute Zero°. The animals in their papers morph into (and out of) other forms: deer emerge out of twigs and swallows fly in and out of leaves, visually merging in a very graphic, almost Escher-like, way. The borders of the wallpaper are, quite literally, defined by their designs, as the groupings of figures running down the edges of the papers become stripes down the wall.

On a more human theme, in German designer Birgit Amadori's wallpapers women have become the central decoration; larger than life and stylised they look as if they might have adorned the walls of a 1960s fashion boutique. These papers are site-specific, exclusively designed to turn each room into a unique environment. The wallpapers from Ten and Don tell a very different story. At first glance, *Archetype Wallpaper Number 1* looks innocuous, but up close turns out to be a pornographic fantasy of a design, with cowboys simulating fellatio. It is somehow more shocking to come across pornographic images on walls; its permanence makes the subject matter totally explicit and incredibly impactful.

## Absolute Zero°

Kenneth Stephenson was new to wallpaper when he founded Absolute Zero° six years ago. His *Seasons* series, commissioned by Places and Spaces in 2004, revealed an acute sense of classic wallpaper patterning and contemporary fashion alertness.

This range of papers features patterns made from images of nature and seasonal transformation. Bees and butterflies diffuse out of honeycomb in the paper designed for the Summer season, while deer leap from a forest of bare trees in Winter, and autumn leaves merge into images of migrating swallows in Autumn, the piece that was most widely acclaimed when it came out in 2004.

These works, like the MC Escher drawings they make reference to, create a electric meeting of the organic and the geometric, with natural forms twisting in and out of symmetrical patterns. These designs seem to resemble fractal formations which draw attention to the mathematical regularity and homogeneity underlying plant and animal shapes. This tension produces a sleek, modern design, which explores the graphic language of pattern, pairing a mathematical symmetry with the vital energy of nature. His *Playtime* series, designed for children, continues this concept of geometry but tones it down with repeating block patterns on pastel backgrounds.

The wallpaper is printed on 80 year old machinery by highly skilled print technicians. They blend the colours by eye, using china clay, which is added to the paint. This gives them a noticeably rich feel. A natural degree of movement in the roller ensures that the end result has a unique, hand-printed quality.

1  *Deer* swatch, from the *Season* inspired range, 2004.
2  *Dandies* detail, from the *Season* inspired range, 2005.
3  *Swallow* swatch, from the *Season* inspired range, 2003.
4  *Bees* swatch, from the *Season* inspired range, 2004.
5  *Knock* swatch, from the *Playtime* range, 2006.
6  *Battery Square* swatch, from the *Playtime* range, 2006.
7  *Sixone*, from the *Playtime* range, 2006.
8  *Town* swatch, from the *Playtime* range, 2006.
9  *Deer*, in situ.
10  *Swallows*, in situ.
11  *3 Kids Outdoors*, from the *Playtime* range, 2006.

9

10

11

# Lizzie Allen

Lizzie Allen is an exciting and innovative young designer with a distinctive and whimsical signature style. After working for several companies, she was awarded funding by the Crafts Council to set up her own business. Allen specialises in producing quality, hand-printed wallpaper and fabrics, often featuring designs with a distinctly British flavour. Take her *London City Gents* paper, with its humorous, quirky line drawings of rotund, suited gents. The hastening figures carry huge newspapers, stout umbrella or briefcases, capturing the spirit of the city with their serious expressions and purposeful strides. Allen's use of colour is unusual and effective, the splashes of mustard yellows and lime greens draw the eye around the design.

Lizzie Allen offers a bespoke service, and often collaborates with architects, art consultants and interior designers to produce commissions specific to a domestic or corporate space. Her wallpapers and fabrics are produced in small batches or made to order. In many cases, she uses embroidery and applique to embellish her designs. This gives her work a personal, individual feel that is very appealing, as exemplified in her *Changing the Guards* print.

There is a clear sense of place in all of Allen's work; her portrayals primarily of Britain, but also of France, resemble illustrations of these places as depicted in children's books. The witty caricatures of objects, furniture and people lend an energy and vitality to the designs, and imbue them with an eccentric, almost wistful appeal that is fun and contemporary.

1 *London City Gents*, hand screen-printed wallpaper, from the *London* collection, 2006.
2 *Hobby-horse Bicycles*, hand screen-printed wallpaper, 2004.
3 *London City Gents* (detail).
4 *Le Petit Waltz*, a hand-printed fabric, which Allen intends to turn into a wallpaper.

Opposite:
*Changing Guards at Buckingham Palace*, hand screen-printed wallpaper from the *London* collection, 2006.

3

1

2

4

# Birgit Amadori

German illustrator Birgit Amadori produces her representational wallpaper using a computer technique called vector illustration. This method involves drawing curves and shapes which are translated by the computer into mathematical algorithms. Each line can be redrawn crisply and precisely at any resolution without the pixellated, digital look often associated with computer art. The clean hard lines that result can often have a similar feel to animated cartoons or children's illustrations.

Since Birgit's designs look good at any scale it was only natural that she would eventually be covering entire walls with her work. She recently designed rooms and stairwells for the Hotel Fox in Copenhagen. More murals than simple wallpaper, her designs for the hotel are monochrome fantasy landscapes which look like Pre-Raphaelite canvases but executed in her inimitable graphic style. The subject matter may be Western European but here her manga and anime influences come to the fore. Her two colour schemes one in cobalt blue and one in blood red, are muted enough so that her characters blend into the forest of the wall as if through a mist.

These monochrome pallets, which are mirrored in the beds and carpet, bathe the hotel in a rich ambiance without the aide of tacky coloured lights. Her total control over the design of a space is the realisation of the *Gestamtkunstwerk* which was the ultimate goal of Art Nouveau and Modernist architects alike. The guests of the Hotel Fox become characters in the fairytale landscapes of her work.

Amadori currently lives in California, and continues to be influenced by the simple and often sinister stories of fairytales and children's literature. Her work has been featured both in galleries and in corporate environments. The folk memories that they evoke are devoid of nostalgia and are globally accessible and admired.

1

2

3

4

5

1  *Hotel Fox Wallpaper*, digital print, 2005.
2  *Hotel Fox, Room 509*, digital print, 2005.
3  *Hotel Fox Wallpaper*, digital print, 2005.
4  *Hotel Fox, Room 217*, digital print, 2005.
5  *Hotel Fox Wallpaper*, digital print, 2005.

## Deborah Bowness

Deborah Bowness' wallpaper does more
than cover walls, it populates rooms with
ethereal readymade objects like mirrors,
chairs and hanging clothes printed directly
on the paper. At first glance, these objects
read as completely plausible fixtures in
a room but a closer look reveals them to
be monochromatic screen prints, which
actually play up the flatness of the medium.
The result is ghostly copies of everyday
things, which fill up rooms without taking
up any space.

These versatile wall-coverings are
available in wall-length strips or can be
purchased in kits—sheets of individual
elements like mirrors and shoes, which
can be cut out and placed at the owner's
discretion. The papers are hand-finished so
they can be tailored to fit any colour scheme.

Her most famous work, *Hooks and Frocks*,
is currently in the Victoria and Albert
Museum's print collection and depicts
jackets seemingly hanging from hooks
in the wall. Another print with an antique
chair is disarmingly real when strategically
placed alone in the corner of a room
but becomes completely surreal when
it is repeated like a pattern along the walls.
*The Genuine Fake Bookshelf* reads as an
imposing bookshelf but also acts like
a very geometric wallpaper pattern.

Whilst a lot of decorative wallpapers
try to take us away from our daily grind
by suggesting jungle landscapes through
patterns, or nature though detached
and repeated images of flowers and birds,
Bowness' work grounds us in the very rooms
we inhabit by by mirroring the household
objects within them, thus blurring the
boundaries between the two-dimensional
wall and the three-dimensional space
around it.

1

2

3

4

5

1 *Patterned Illusion* in red from the *Illusions of Grandeur* collection.
2 *Salon Chair*, from the *Salvage* Collection.
3 *Salon Chair* in corridor.
4 *Original Genuine Fake Bookshelf*, in Soho House, London.
5 *Patterned Illusion* in brown from the *Illusions of Grandeur* collection.

# Erotic Dragon

Erotic Dragon is the brainchild of Miho Sadowaga, and is characterised by vivid colours, strong motifs and an illustrative style. Her work has a strong Asian influence and is powerfully informed by Japanese pop culture. She has been commissioned to produce several wallpapers, the first of which was for Cafe Croiser, located in the Mitsukoshi department store in Ginza. The cafe is a haven from the clamour and consumerism of the store, and Sadowaga has created a snug corner using a cheerful palette of warm yellow, ochre, and evocative saffron and amber tones. The impression is of a radiant and reviving sunset, emphasised by the gentle graduation of tones across the wall. On this sun-drenched background bloom massive lotus flowers whose petals echo and harmonise with the blazing sunset colours. The lotus is a motif renowned for its associations with purity and serenity, and the giant flowers provide visual interest for diners without being overpowering or busy.

In *Navigator of Paradise*, a mysterious female figure is featured interwoven with sinuous stalks and strands of flowers and plants. The design is like an illustration from an exotic fairytale, and indeed Sadowaga says of the work: "I imagined capturing items that appear in the world of Erotic Dragon... there is a kind of story that I have created... and I made a design that might exist in the background of that story."

Erotic Dragon also produces more subdued, ornamental designs, as illustrated in *Tapestry*. This design has an almost Art Deco feel, albeit with an Asian slant, and features highly stylised flowers in bold colours. These are entwined with sweeping, curving lines, referencing classic wallpaper design yet remaining fresh, contemporary and characteristic of Erotic Dragon's quirky, eastern-influenced work.

1

2

3

1-3 Details from *Untitled*, print on wallpaper fabric, wallpaper installation at the Mitsukoshi department store, Tokyo, 2005.
4 *Tapestry*, 2005.
5 *Navigator of Paradise*, exclusively for the Maxalot Wallpaper Project, 2005.

4

5

# Nama Rococo

Nama Rococo, founded by Karen Combs, takes its name from from its birthplace— North Adams Massachussetts, combined with the the old-school sensuousness of Rococo. Combs cites a variety of influences on her unique designs—including traditional Chinese designs, Art Nouveau and Funkadelic album covers.

The *French Dot* design features one of a kind watercolour-like washes painted by hand and overlaid with a bold pen and ink style pattern. The colour scheme is playfully referred to as 'Ooh-La Black'. *Serious BoKay* functions like a traditional diamond pattern but these geometric shapes are actually made out of clusters of cottony cloud-like objects. The diamonds are carefully staggered to break up the rigid lines, which would otherwise cut across the wall. *Tokyo Vine* is a minimal and elegant floral pattern on day-glo pink, which betrays their penchant for Japanese design.

The colours in all of Nama Rococo wallpapers are key to their composition. Combs describes it like a symphony: "Sound is form, tone is colour. We take flowing, lively shapes and knock them curiously off kilter. Colours, luminous and rich are made to dance across the paper and into the living space."

Intended for large spaces like lofts which can often be cold and anonymous, these designs bring a welcome warmth and a sense of fun to the modern urban environment.

1  *Tokyo & Vine* in flourescent cerise, hand-screened over freehand painted ground using artists pigments on acid-free paper, 2006.
2  *French Dot* in Ooh La Black, hand-screened over freehand painted ground using artists pigments on acid-free paper, 2006.
3  *Serious Bokay* in black and white, hand-screened over freehand painted ground using artists pigments on acid-free paper, 2006.

1

2

3

# Nice

Nice is the brainchild of British designers Sofie Eliasson and Matt Duckett. Their wallpaper ranges play with repeating patterns using strictly unconventional forms. Their popular *Hybrid* wallpaper consists of silhouettes of giraffes, horses, crickets, sharks and lobsters whose front and back ends can be rearranged into every possible combination. The range includes three basic rolls, each with a set of animal fronts and backs which when hung side by side can yield countless species of mutants, which the home-owner can mix and match as he/she desires. This highly conceptual piece of interior design reads surprisingly well as wallpaper, but is not for the shy retiring type of interior—the *Hybrid* range refuses to blend into the background; its endless variation invites inspection and becomes a focal point for any room.

Eliasson and Duckett work in a variety of mediums as well as wallpaper, including illustration and graphic design. With all their products they try and introduce the playful humour evident in their wallpaper.

*Hybrid* wallpaper, 2005.

## Ten and Don

Inspired by the cowboy-themed wallpaper of their childhood, Ten and Don have taken a maverick approach to contemporary wallpaper design. They point out that "Children used to be children, whereas today they are small grown-ups—and the big guys crave for the romantic memories from their childhood." Filling this void in the modern psyche, these designers have fashioned a nostalgic design using modern techniques. Ten and Don attempt to imitate the look and feel of older papers and their more limited printing techniques by choosing slightly skewed colours. The cowboy design looks faded by years in a child's bedroom.

Their wallpaper resembles the quintessential boys' bedroom wallpaper adorned with cowboys, builders or truck drivers yet Ten and Don capitalise on the homosexual subtext of these images of men in the company of men. The two figures lounge against a fence wearing unbuttoned shirts, bushy mustaches and crotchless chaps. Next to them are two ejaculating six-shooters and the words "Cum and Join". Sinuey lassoos literally tie the composition together.

Ten and Don's commitment to the traditional wallpaper format and repeating patterns brings the irony of the composition into stark relief.

*Archetype Wallpaper Number 1, 2005.*

# William Wegman

William Wegman is one of the most established artists working in wallpaper today. Wegman first emerged onto the 1970s New York art scene, collaborating with Man Ray on a number of photographic and video installations. He went on to branch into children's books and animation, although his most famous work has been a series of humorous photographs of his Weimaraner dogs, which have been exhibited in galleries and published in numerous books. The Surrealist roots he started from are never very far from his work.

Wegman first turned his hand to wallpaper design in the early 1990s, having completed a series of playfully decorative prints, that he and publisher Elisabeth Cunnick realised would fit the medium well. *Activities* makes reference to a wholesome New England lifestyle. The wallpaper comprises rudimentary inkblots, which at first seem randomly decorative, but at a closer glance appear oddly tribal—the sketches resembling primitive cave drawings—and only upon close examination, do we realise that we are looking at an idyllic vision of the great outdoors. The inkblots form themselves before our eyes into boys canoeing, fishing and sitting by a campfire.

*Alphabet Border* also first existed as single photo studio pieces that were later adapted for wallpaper. Here we see his well-known Weimaraner dogs, hilariously formed into alphabet shapes, famously recalling the nineteenth century English pictorial alphabets. Each photograph was colour-separated so that every letter could be cast in a different warm or cool tone of Weimaraner grey.

Below:
*Activities,* 1993.

Opposite:
*Alphabet Border,* 1993.

# Hanna Werning

Whether it be classic monochrome, floral chic or folkish, fairy-tale imagery of forests and woodlands, Hanna Werning's prints boast bold, clearly articulated designs. Her work marries technology and craft. In *Electric Jungle*, digital printed cloth is embellished with cross stitch in an intricate and meticulous patterning. In Apparat No. *1*, a drawing machine used black permanent markers to create patterns at random repeat.

This hi-fi low-fi dichotomy is further explored with the formats of her mass-produced wallpaper. Rather than packaging her work in rolls, as is customary, Werning designs many of her wallpapers as posters. The decorator has the choice to past a number of sheets together to cover a wall or to use them as individual prints. These brightly coloured papers are dense collages of plant and creature silhouettes layered together as free-floating graphic elements.

Often the shapes are taken out of context, such as her pairing of seahorses with pumas and jungle plants. Deer skip freely across a scape of magnified palm leaves. These saturated designs are oddly subtle and peaceful, despite the initial, frenetic impression that they make.

A Swedish native, Hanna studied graphic design at Central St Martins College in London. She has worked in both print and moving image design, as well as developed a range of textiles. Her first wallpaper in rolls has recently been produced with Swedish wallpaper manufacturer Bor Stapeter.

Hannah sees her work as falling under two categories: designs that are driven by ideas, and those that are intuitively driven by colour and rhythm. We can see both aspects at play in her iconic wallpaper motifs of flowers and birds sleekly incorporated into lively colour fields.

1 *Black Kite*, from the *AnimalFlowers* wallpaper-posters collection, litho on blue-back paper 2001–2004.
2 *Ekorreblad*, from the *AnimalFlowers* wallpaper-posters collection, litho on blue-back paper 2001–2004.
3 *Djurträdgård*, from the *AnimalFlowers* wallpaper-posters collection, litho on blue-back paper 2001–2004.
4 *Krokodillöv*, from the *AnimalFlowers* wallpaper-posters collection, litho on blue-back paper 2001–2004.
5 *Sjöhästäng*, from the *AnimalFlowers* wallpaper-posters collection, litho on blue-back paper 2001–2004.
6 *Zebraskog*, from the *AnimalFlowers* wallpaper-posters collection, litho on blue-back paper 2001–2004.

Overleaf left:
*Flodhästvår*, from the *AnimalFlowers* wallpaper-posters collection, litho on blue-back paper 2001–2004.

Overleaf right:
*Ekorreblad*, from the *AnimalFlowers* wallpaper-posters collection, litho on blue-back paper 2001–2004.

1

2

3

4

5

6

# Wook Kim

Graphic artist, painter and installation artist, Wook Kim, plays with our perceptions of wallpaper, by using traditional patterns and motifs, and inserting into their midst unexpected animals at odd intervals. In *Priori*, a unicorn peers up at the ceiling. The title of the piece is a witty observation of the ways in which we qualify our knowledge through experience rather than faith. In *Ironmonkey*, the foliage turns from being merely a decorative motif to a literal representation, thanks to the little monkey, searching his way through the leaves.

The animals often seem lost; adrift in the relentless patterning around them. Their stylised features make them seem strange and exotic—aliens in foreign lands; innocent intruders in a sea of repetition. Wook Kim's background is in textile design, and his understanding of depth within a two dimensional medium is clearly apparent. The shadows of the foliage in *Ironmonkey* make the little ape even more conspicuous in his two-dimensional flatness.

The wallpapers are digitally printed in limited print runs. Kim tries to stay away from mass-production, believing that society is already overly obsessed with consumerism. In his own words: "My interest in materials such as paper, light and sound have to do with ideas of non-permanence, qualities of decomposing or passing. The quality of passage sets us in a place within space that creates an understanding of the preciousness of a moment."

1,2  *Cabbage*, digitally printed in a limited edition, 2004.
3-5  *Bayou*, digitally printed in a limited edition, 2004.
6-8  *Lis*, digitally printed in a limited edition, 2004.
9,10  *Priori*, digitally printed in a limited edition, 2004.
11  *Iron Monkey*, *Priori*, digitally printed in a limited edition, 2004.
12-14  *Jacob*, digitally printed in a limited edition, 2004.

Overleaf left:
*Iron Monkey*, digitally printed in a limited edition, 2004.

Overleaf right:
*Priori*, digitally printed in a limited edition, 2004.

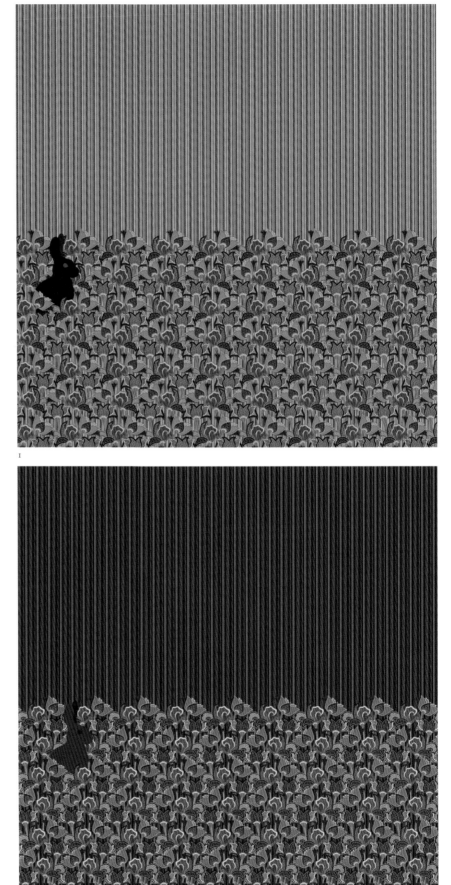

1

2

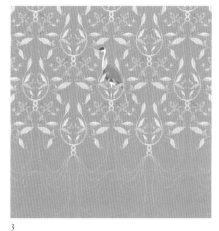

3

4

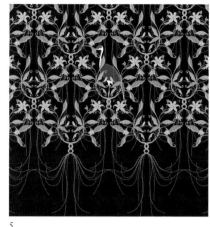

5

6

7

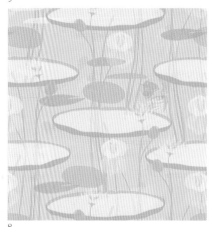

8

9

10

11

12

13

14

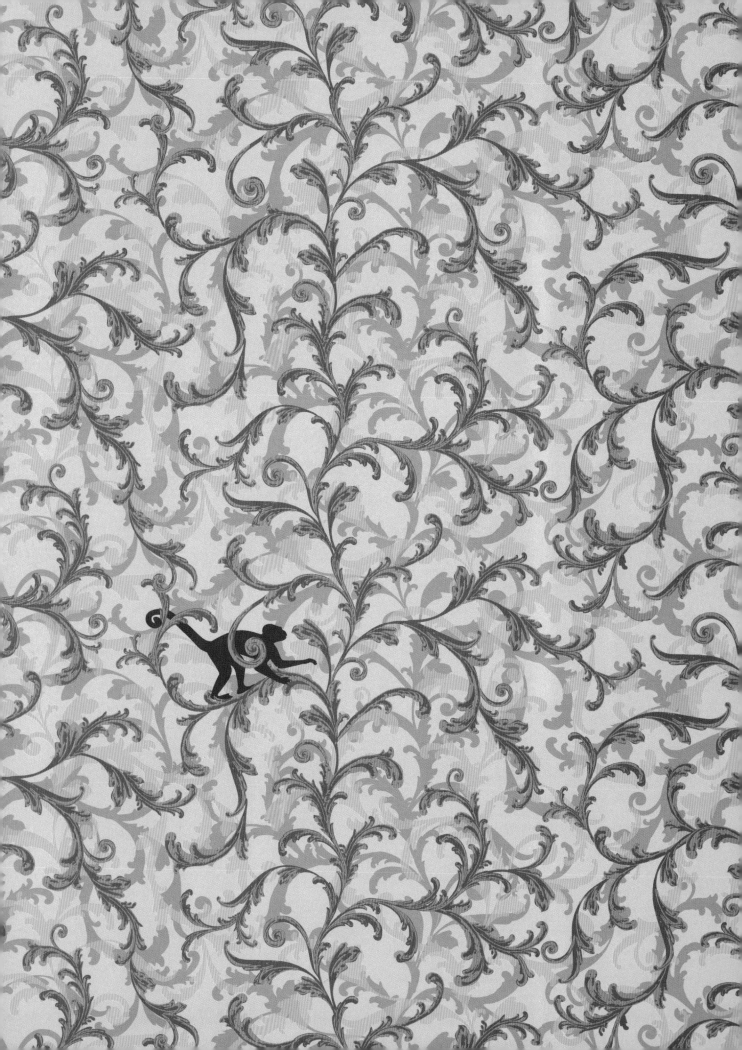

Abstract and Geometric

Abstract patterned wallpapers have their origins in the geometric papers produced in the 1930s. The non-figurative, graphic and Art Deco patterns that were so prevalent across the fine and applied arts then opened the consumers' eye up to less traditional shapes and colours. The Modernist movement, whose origins were strongly associated with Germany and the Bauhaus School, produced some very striking art, textiles and patternings. Though wallpaper was not high on the Modernist agenda, the patterns that came out of the movement were extremely popular and extensively copied.

Similarly the work of abstract painters like Klee, Miro and Mondrian were plundered for commercial ends. In France, designers working for couture fashion houses were some of the first to produce sumptuous patterns for textiles and wallpapers; the latter often designed for use in fashion boutiques. The American market was instrumental in appropriating catwalk fashion for mass produced textiles and wallpapers. In the English market, the use of abstract wallpaper patterns in the 1930s was often confined to decorative borders, but the potential had been created, and by the 1950s the use of abstract wallpaper designs was more confidently widespread. Much has been made of the Festival of Britain and its accompanying 'molecular' patterns, influenced by scientific advances. The patterns of Lucienne Day—abstracted symbols of everyday life—opened up the market for designed wallpapers, rather than simply decorative ones. By the 1960s wallpaper came in vibrant geometric patterns, shapes, stripes and colours, crystallising ideas of abstract wallpaper design.

Contemporary abstract wallpapers still have something of the 1960s about them. It is for this reason that there is a flourishing market for collecting original textiles and wallpapers from this period. Contemporary designers have an appreciation of the possibilities of abstract wallpapers to modernise a space, and many have utilised the computer for to introduce a random element and open up wild possibilities for digital manipulation. The Anglo-Brazilian fashion designers Basso & Brooke have brought a truly twenty-first century motif to this abstract genre. At a distance, their computer-generated wallpapers look to be almost Arts and Crafts patterns, but up close their characteristic intricacy and peculiar pixellations give the papers a much more edgy abstraction, producing a combination of reference characteristic of contemporary wallpaper design. Dan Funderburgh is producing wallpapers that have a more explicit pattern, but from a distance they are still abstract, combining the domestic with the edgy in order to play with our expectations. Drawing upon the past and delivering designs that could only have been produced, technically speaking, in the present, Funderburgh provides us with designs for the future.

# Johanna Basford

Johanna Basford's work is inspired by the wildlife and nature that surrounds her, her studio being based at a fish farm in Aberdeenshire, Scotland. Delicate hand-drawings of imagined botanicals, teeming with curious beasts and butterflies, are used to re-invent traditional Victorian motifs. The designs are then translated onto paper using traditional silk-screen printing. The result is a tactile and intricate print, conveying all the unique qualities of the original hand-drawings.

The monochrome wallpapers are available in the signature black and white collection as well as a selection of colours and finishes, such as gloss, flock and metallic. These rich and luxurious colours and textures are rendered practically weightless by her airy patterns. Johanna also creates bespoke designs, specially commissioned by the customer. Her commitment to unique and personal wallpaper allows her to convey the delicate tangles of nature and enhances the intimacy of the home.

In Basford's own words: "I believe design should be organic and that the designer's hand-print should be interlaced throughout the piece. By using hand-drawn motifs and images, I try to capture both the natural essence that inspired the print, but also my own personal involvement with the piece. I aim to capture the beauty of nature and to translate it into designs which enrich our environment."

1

1  *Insectiana 2*, silkscreen printed wallpaper, black on white, 2006.
2  *Crazy Botanic*, detail, silkscreen printed wallpaper, black on white, 2006.
3  *Crazy Botanic*, detail, silkscreen printed wallpaper, black on white, 2006.
4  *Fish-To-Fly*, pen and ink drawing for wallpaper design, 2006.

2

3

# Basso & Brooke

Basso & Brooke's 'power prints' are not for the shy interiors; each one a pulsating world of fantasy graphics and surrealist flourishes. Titles like *Alchemy*, *Age of Enlightenment* and *Eureka* make reference to graphic novels, science-fiction narratives and fairytales. The monochrome *Solaris* is comprised of Lewis Carroll style illustrations of the weird and wonderful, centring on images of 'travel and exploration'. It seems to spin a mysterious fable but the result is darker and denser than the traditional children's nursery-rhyme wallpaper.

Each of their works is a frenzy of symbols and motifs, often reminiscent of the outrageous, meticulously detailed landscapes of Hieronymus Bosch. The play of bright comic book colours against more subtle machine greys gives the papers a haphazard cut and paste feel, while the intricate patterns and precise gradients suggest the aid of a computer and in places, recalls the graphics of 16-bit side-scrolling computer games. This 1980s aesthetic, coupled with the 1970s inspired hallucinogenic aspect of the design, means that Basso & Brooke wallpaper is at once retro, and undeniably contemporary.

The unorthodox duo, Chris Brooke, hailing from Nottingham, and Bruno Basso, from Brazil, met at Popstarz nightclub in London, in 2002. Like so many wallpaper designers, their background is in fashion and textiles and they have produced similarly wild collections for Ferretti, Moschino and Jean Paul Gaultier, as well as commissions for numerous celebrities.

1

1 *Alchemy*, digital print, Autumn/Winter 2006.
2 *Succubus Adventure*, digital print, Autumn/Winter 2005.
3 *Eureka*, digital print, Autumn/Winter 2006.
4 *Solaris*, digital print, Spring/Summer 2006.
5 *Poodle Portrait*, digital print, Spring/Summer 2006.

Overleaf left:
*Hollywood*, digital print, spring/summer 2006.

Overleaf right:
*Age of Enlightenment*, digital print, Autumn/Winter 2006.

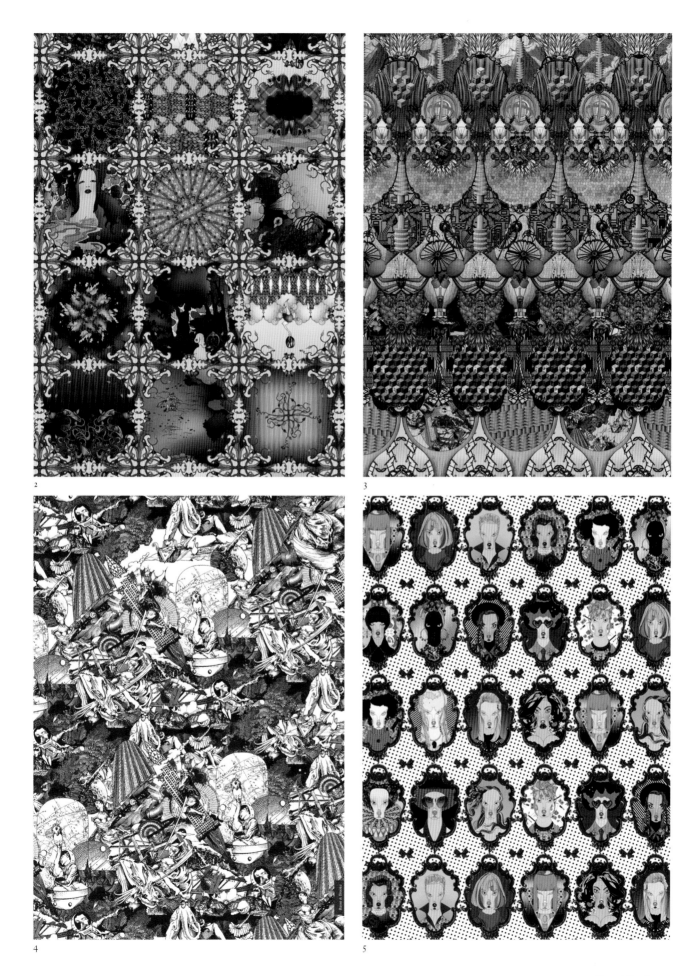

2

3

4

5

## Markus Benesch

Markus Benesch is primarily concerned, like
so many designers before him, with the poetic
side of design. Whilst others concentrate
on new processes or purely practical works,
Benesch continues to use interior design as a
means of personal expression. His installation
*La Casa di Alice* is a total environment in
which his colourful images spill off the walls
and cover everything from the floor to all the
furniture and appointments. Taking its name
from the Lewis Carroll book, *La Casa* is
a disorienting psychedelic journey through
everyday spaces. Benesch uses colour and
shape to dematerialise the walls and make the
space entirely fluid. He explains that circles
can be used as axis points in space to virtually
redraw the room, denying its actual
boundaries. The over-saturated colours
on the walls read spatially and confuse
the delineations of the room. Similarly,
the furniture, covered in laminate of the same
pattern dissolve into the whole rather than
competing with it. In one room, a mirrored
staircase emphasises this confusion between
the two- and three-dimensional.

One of his wall designs features bold
interweaving concentric circles which, like
the famous optical illusion, seem to spin
of their own accord. Other designs take
their cues from 1960s Op Art and use skewed
patterns to seemingly bend the wall. This
juxtaposition of colours and patterns make
his rooms a more optical than spatial
experience. Although not for the faint of
heart, Markus's rooms are a bold statement
of purpose. His unflinching and relentless
barrage of colour forces us to take notice
of the way we relate to the spaces and realities
that we inhabit.

1  *Horizon Suave and Lip Effect*, from the
   *Colorflage by Rasch* collection, 2004.
2  *Sky Red* from the *Colorflage by Rasch*
   collection, 2004.
3  Detail from *La Casa Di Alice*, installation
   at the Post Design gallery, Milan, 2005.
4  *Horizon Multi with Twist Effect* and
   L-type furniture in Flow Dot magenta
   laminate, from the *Colorflage by Rasch*
   collection, 2004.
5  *Black and White Flow Dots*, from the
   *Colorflage by Rasch* collection, 2004.
6  *Neonite* from the *Colorflage by Rasch*
   collection, 2004.
7  *Horizon Suave with Lip Effect*, detail.
8, 9  *Black and White Flow Dots*, detail.

1

2

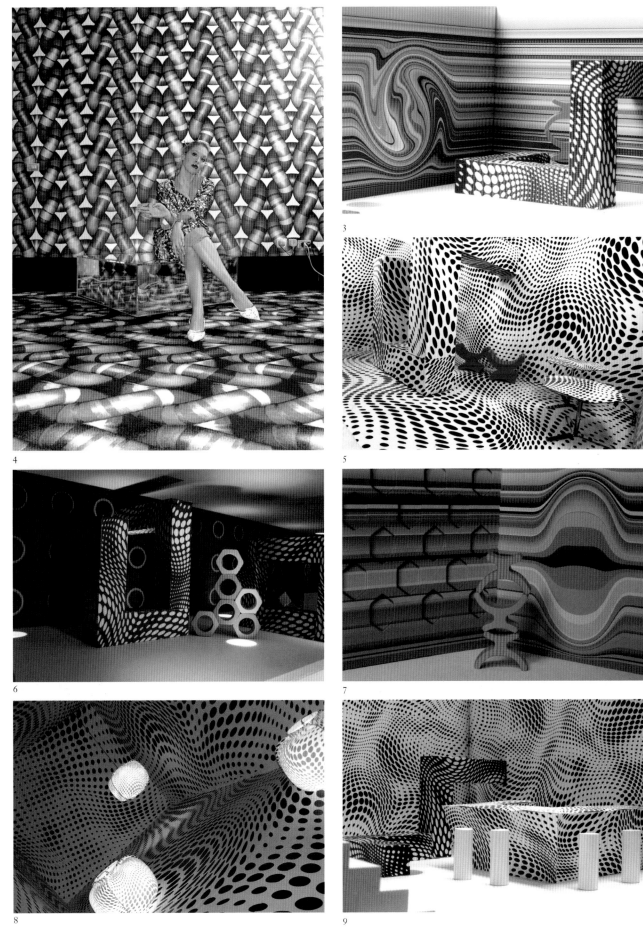

4

3

5

6

7

8

9

# Committee

The prolific design duo Committee have a talent for turning other peoples junk into iconic pieces of interior design. Clare Page and Harry Richardson were recently recognised for their Kebab Lamps which skewer sculpted bits of trash on a floor lamp pole. The objects have a glossy, toy-like appearance, which removes them from any junk connotations. In the spirit of Pop Art, these designers celebrate the commercial objects which make up the foliage of our urban jungle. Their work doesn't glorify kitsch, it celebrates the way everyday things like shoes and teddy bears can be imbued with a personal significance. Their *Flytip* wallpaper, which was ironically hand-printed by the very traditional Cole & Son, features a swirling tornado of bric-a-brac found in the stalls of London's Deptford Market near

their studio. Far from being random, these objects are carefully selected and arranged; only their juxtaposition gives the impression of rubbish. The column of objects can be applied horizontally or vertically as an isolated strip on a sky-blue background—a very unique compositional element in a room.

A similar project, *Breakthrough*, involves a *trompe-l'oeil* hole in the paper through which a deluge of trash is flowing. The varying scale of the objects and the mix of three-dimensional and two-dimensional items makes for a surreal effect. This design rejects traditional repeating patterns, drawing attention to itself by virtue of its dynamic explosiveness. These are accents rather than motifs and they suggest new possibilities for the use of wallpaper in the design of a room.

Below:
*Breakthrough*, hand-printed by Cole & Son, 2005.

Opposite:
*Flytip*, hand-printed by Cole & Son, 2005.

# Dominic Crinson

UK designer Dominic Crinson's work retains the baroque ornateness of more traditional wallpaper but discards the traditional motifs in favour of bold, jagged and contemporary patterns. He is best known for his work with digital print tiles, which have been used much like wallpaper to adorn the walls of Heathrow Airport and The Big Chill Bar in London. These versatile tiles can be used to coat a wall in a repeating pattern or mixed and matched to create a unique mosaic effect or even pieced together to form a large-scale digital mural.

Crinson's wallpaper designs are clearly informed by work with tiles. His compositions are often based on square motifs. Axial symmetry within the squares is often employed to distort recognisable images like clouds and flowers as if through a kaleidoscope. In the *Faux Rococo* range, this reliance on a rigid grid system is used to tame fairly chaotic and unwieldy patterns. These opulent and dense designs are made out of extreme and sometimes clashing colour combinations, which at a distance, create an overall neutral effect.

*Clouded*, is a clever kaleidoscoping of clouds, to create a geometric pattern out of the clouds' random shapes. *Kitchenset* is an uncharacteristically hand-drawn jumble of cookery set against a vibrant red and orange background. This eclectic body of work is unified by Crinson's acute sense of rhythm and seriality and clever subversions of conventional wallpaper styles.

1  *Chou Mauve 3* from the *Incredible Edibles Collection*, digitally printed wallpaper, 2002.
2  *Blue Glitz 3* from the *Glitz Collection*, digitally printed wallpaper, 2002.
3  *Jantar B11* from the *Jantar Mantar Collection*, digitally printed wallpaper, 2004.
4  *Kitchenset* from the *Sketch Collection*, digitally printed wallpaper, 2001.
5  *Woodit 11* from the *Extreme Collection*, digitally printed wallpaper, 2003.
6  *Clouded 7* from the *Extreme Collection*, digitally printed wallpaper, 2005.

1

2

3

4

5

6

# Dan Funderburgh

Dan Funderburgh's absurd and politically
conscious designs have won him the rapt
attention of the New York design community.
His baroque-like patterns are embedded
with kitschy household objects like plastic
milk cartons, 40 ounce bottles and cartoons,
which are given a strange sophistication
by being included in such classic patterns.
Funderburgh's bold Technicolor palette
make his images jump off the wall, worlds
away from traditional muted wallcoverings.

Funderburgh is the co-founder of
Thought Ninjas of North America, and has
worked closely with various skate apparel
companies—the influence of which is evident
throughout his work. Patterns like *Loose
Cannon* are baroque fractals constructed
out of cannon fire, grenades and horseshoes.
*Death from Above* is a witty reinterpretation
of Magritte's *Golconde* in which the
anonymous flying men in bowler hats are
replaced by flying kitchen utensils. *Dependence
Day* is a striking gradient made up of little
dollar shaped rectangles, which read '$17.76';
a not so subtle jab at both American
nationalism and consumerism.

Funderburgh was born and raised
in Mid-West America, and has an acute
awareness of the privileges of upbringing
and education that he was privy to. By using
wallpaper to convey political messages,
Funderburgh literally brings home the
issues that we need to concern ourselves
with, and allows no room for denial or escape.
His utilisation of repeating patterns is in
itself a comment on the way we can immunise
ourselves to the atrocities of the world around
us. The blend of urban, skate, and low-art
iconography, makes his walls an active rather
than a passive element of any room.

1

1  *Hold East Skateboard*, digital print, 2005.
2  2005 *Living Spaces Design Showcase*,
   digital print, 2005.
3  *Homefront*, digital print, 2005.
4  *Manhattan Storage*, screenprint, 2004.
5  *B&E*, digital print, 2005.

Overleaf left:
*Death from Above*, digital print, 2006.

Overleaf right:
*Dependence Day*, digital print, 2005.

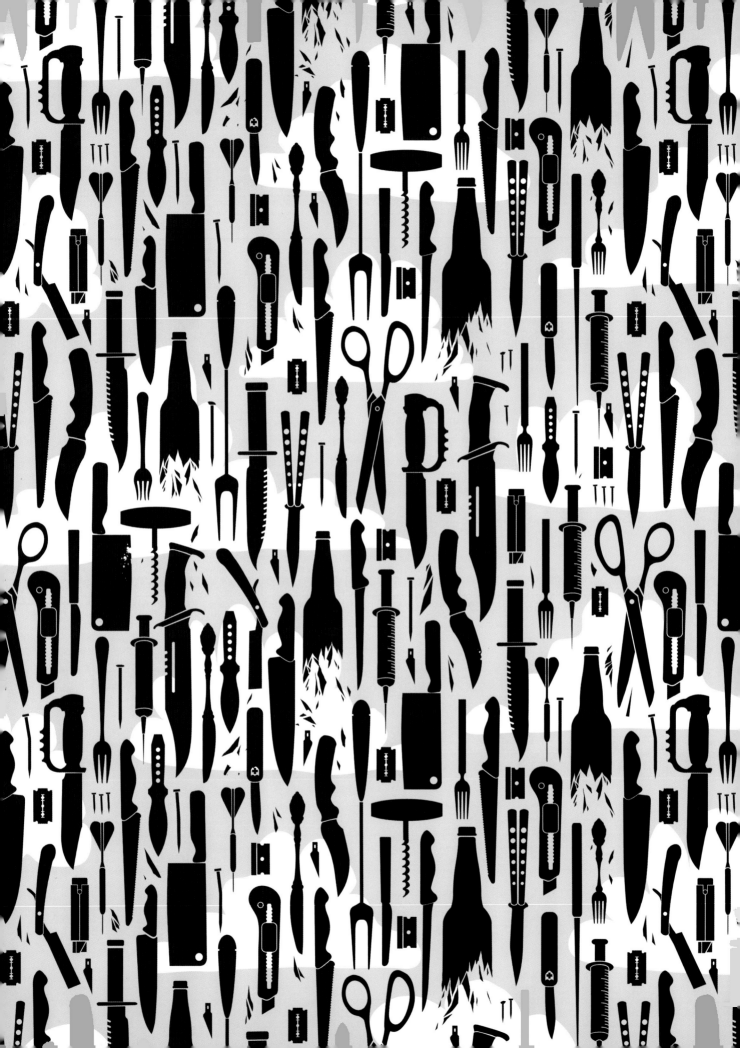

# Jane Masters

Jane Masters is a British born artist living and working in the United States. Like so many artists working with wallpaper, the capacity of wallpaper to cover large spaces is central to her choice of medium. Using intricate and labour intensive working methods including hand-drawing, silk-screening and wood-burning, her work creates a dialogue between scale and detail. The precise repetitive product is at once serenely meditative and bordering on the neurotic.

In her installation *Dougal and Zebedee Discuss Geometry*, which was exhibited at the De Cordova Museum in Massachussetts, Masters uses an abstract repeating wallpaper pattern, painstakingly hand-printed in individual sheets, and hung to create a seamless single pattern. On top of this are hung detailed scratchboard drawings, of black ink on kaolin, at precise intervals. They look as though they could be computer-generated magnifications of the wallpaper patterning, and yet, this is precisely the opposite of the truth.

In her wallpaper panels *Obsessive Compulsive*, Masters uses a wood-burning tool to singe thousands of tiny holes in large sheets of white drawing paper. The effect is reminiscent of 1960s flock, and with their folksy, floral decoration there is a definite kitsch aspect to the series. However, the words at the centre of the panels; 'oops' 'obsessive' 'control freak'—create an ironic self-awareness of both the process and the product.

1 *Groovy: Version 4*, a wallpaper piece for *On the Wall: Contemporary Wallpaper*, a show at the Museum of the Rhode Island School of Design, 2003.
2 *Groovy: Version 4* in situ.
3 View of two burnt drawings installed on gallery walls, *Obsessive Compulsive* and *Oops!*, burnt paper, Sintra board, paint, acrylic bushings, screws, magnets, 2005.
4 *Control Freak* detail, burnt paper, Sintra board, paint, acrylic bushings, screws, magnets, 2005.
5 Printing *Dougal and Zebedee Discuss Geometry* wallpaper in studio. Lacquer-based inks, on paper, four colours, hand-screened, for installation in the DeCordova Museum and Sculpture Gardens, Lincoln, Massachusetts, 2003.
6 Full view of installation *Dougal and Zebedee Discuss Geometry* with hand-screened wallpaper and scratchboard drawings.

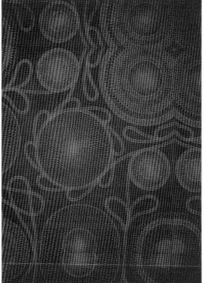

1

2

3

4

5

6

## Virgil Marti

Virgil Marti is known internationally for his shrewd, satirical, witty installations. Taking elements of décor and inserting them into the fine art context, his work focuses on the fascinating interplay between good and bad taste, high and low art.

His work often carries a personal or social significance. Giant pills and beercans cover vast wall spaces, bringing Warhol's concepts firmly into the twenty-first century. *Lotus* is inspired by the textile patterns of Japanese Noh Robes, the history of decorative arts and pop culture of the 1960s and 70s, and takes traditionally decorative floral motifs into new, sinister territory. Perhaps Marti's most famous wallpaper is *Bullies*. This widely exhibited piece is comprised of yearbook photos of actual bullies from Marti's high school. Their faces peer out from 'frames' and are surrounded by a violently fluorescent, psychedelic pattern that demands engagement. The past tormentors are publicly accused, and the viewers are invited to project their own grudges onto the lurid faces. In doing so they are complicit in the vendetta of the artist; the questionable wisdom of this 'naming and shaming' becomes an ethical dilemma that the viewer is forced to grapple with.

Marti explains his attraction to the medium of wallpaper as follows: "I liked the idea of making something you might not recognise immediately as art. Or you might miss it entirely and just see it as wallpaper." By positioning his art within a product, Marti once again mocks the standards by which we judge fine art.

1

2

3

4

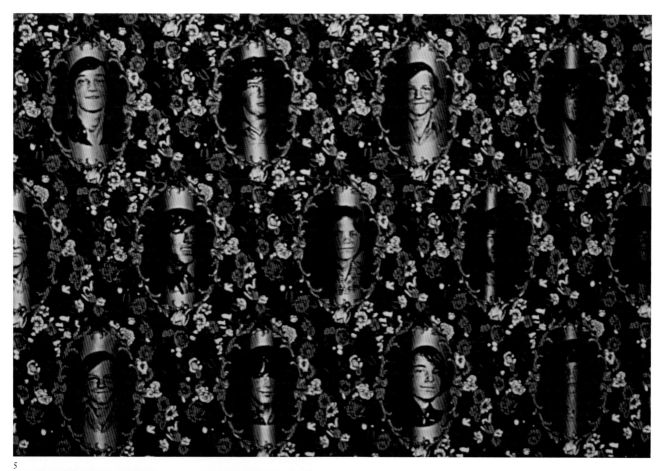

5

6

1 *Lotus Room*, hand screen-pront on Mylar,
 with digital decals, 2003.
2 *Beer Can Library*, four-colour process
 screen-printed wallpaper, installation
 exhibited in *Domestic Diversions*, group
 exhibition, Philadelphia Art Alliance, 1997.
 Photograph by Aaron Igler.
3 Detail from *Beer Can Library*, 1997.
 Photograph by Aaron Igler.
4 *Sleeping Pills*, screen-printed ink and rayon
 flock on paperbacked silver Mylar, 1996.
5 *Bullies*, fluorescent flocked wallpaper,
 blacklights and wooden locker room bench.
 Installation exhibited in *Apocalyptic Wallpaper*
 group exhibition, Wexner Center for the
 Arts, Columbus, Ohio, 1997 (originally
 1992). Photograph by Richard K. Loesch.
6 *For Oscar Wilde*, ceramic plaque, live
 sunflowers, silk lillies, hand-printed
 wallpaper, wood moulding, cotton velveteen
 cover on metal prison bed. Detail from an
 installation exhibited in *Prison Sentences:
 The Prison as Site / The Prison as Subject*,
 Eastern State Penitentiary, Philadelphia,
 1995. Photograph by Will Brown.

# Jorge Pardo

It is hardly a recent phenomenon for wallpaper to stray from the realm of interior design and brave the domain of the contemporary artist. But in the hands of an artist like Jorge Pardo, wallpaper explodes from the flimsy walls of living rooms and hotel lobbies, and runs wild through turbine halls, building exteriors and museums alike with designs that reflect the industrial scale of the space.

Born in Cuba, Jorge Pardo emigrated to the United States where he studied at The Art Center College of Design. He has participated in numerous seminal international group exhibitions and realised major solo and permanent projects that rocked the international art world. His project in Ansicht Turbine Hall features a wide array of colourful, personal and seemingly hand-drawn images which provide a sharp contrast to the monstrous scale and mechanical processes

at work in the space. These playful murals transform the factory environment from industrial age gloom to a vibrant workplace suggesting that designers have the power to restore dignity to labour.

Pardo has worked with exteriors as well as interiors, bringing his playful ideas and frenetic energy to this work as well. A warehouse in Miami is encloaked in lurid camouflage, looking as though it has been attacked by an overzealous graffiti artist. Other wallpaper projects are highly self-conscious takes on the medium; combining cut outs of traditional wallpaper with CGI renderings of random objects and views opening onto computer-generated rooms. His computer-aided design is unabashedly digital and revels in the three-dimensional possibilities of two-dimensional planes.

1 *Untitled* detail, ink-jet print on wallpaper, 2004.
2 *Untitled*, (Turbinenhalle), individually coloured linen fabric in 96 different colours, glazed clay tiles, installed in the Turbine-Hall of the Stadwerke Dusseldorf, 2003.
3 *Untitled*, mural paint, 2006.

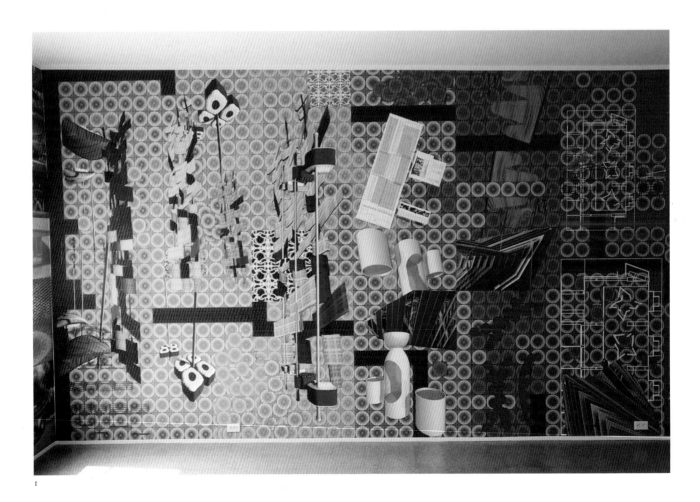

1

2

5

# PSYOP

Comprising five creative partners, PSYOP
is an award-winning design team whose
conceptual approach to project work unites
the disciplines of design, animation and
live-action. Founded in 2000, PSYOP
have since gone on to create visual motion
graphics for the advertising marketing,
video-gaming, broadcast and music video
industries. Their distinct conceptual
approach has culminated in projects for
clients as diverse as Ford, Nike, Red Hot
Chili Peppers, and Volkswagen.

*Frozen Honey* is the only wallpaper design
by the New York based company. Created
especially for the Maxalot Gallery, an
exhibition space based in Barcelona that
aims to showcase graphic design as art,
and to provide a space where artist-designers
can create works without the restriction
of the boundaries that client projects
necessarily entail, PSYOP have produced
a wallpaper that evades easy categorisation.

*Frozen Honey*'s muted pastel colours, soft
lines and painterly aesthetic imbue it with
an ethereal, soothing quality. A kaleidoscope
of pattern and indefinable shapes initially
locate it in an abstract and ambiguous realm,
neither painting nor digital art, which
eludes easy identification. Simultaneously,
however, the hyper-detailed finish pulls
the eye into the artwork, where seductive
pattern and sexual innuendo begin to
emerge. This tension between transparency
and high-finish, a painterly and digital
aesthetic is what gives this work by PSYOP
its distinct multi-disciplinary character.

*Frozen Honey*, for the Maxalot design
showcase, 2005.

# Showroom Dummies

The design group Showroom Dummies, made up of Abigail Lane, Brigitte Stepputtis and Bob Pain, have a talent for turning disturbing and odd imagery into unthreatening and strangely beautiful wall-coverings. The highlight of their 2003 launch show was a room with a wooden fireplace coated in macabre skeleton tiles and surrounded by a mural-sized black and white photo of a volcanic eruption. This freeze frame of nature's fury lends an eerie stillness to the space. Another room featured a cashmere-covered bed with lizards, dogs and bugs flanked on either side by lightning bolts. The electric storm is mirrored on either side of the bed giving it a surreal quality. Despite the initial jolt, this horrific imagery always remains subordinate to Showroom Dummies' sophisticated designs and when incorporated as design elements, these images lose much of their bite. Their taste for predominantly stark black and white motifs is softened by their taste for luxurious and homely materials.

Their *Skeleton* wallpaper and matching chair covers, combine the humorous, the gothic and the contemporary. A model caravan, which they decorated has an uncharacteristically DIY feel but includes recurring themes such as the checkerboard, skulls and coffins, in a more varied colour palette. Other wallpaper designers tend to conceal such controversial images in more traditional forms or smuggle them in along with more innocent fare, but Showroom Dummies flaunt the strange and frightening and somehow manage to domesticate it.

Top right:
*Volcanic Eruption Mural*, London, 2003.
Photograph by Coco Amardeil.

Bottom right:
*Skeleton Wallpaper*, London, 2003.
Photograph by Julian Dodd.

Opposite:
A selection of details from their *Caravan* installation, 2006.

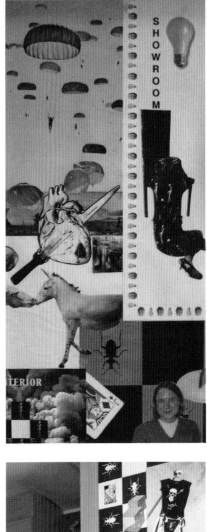

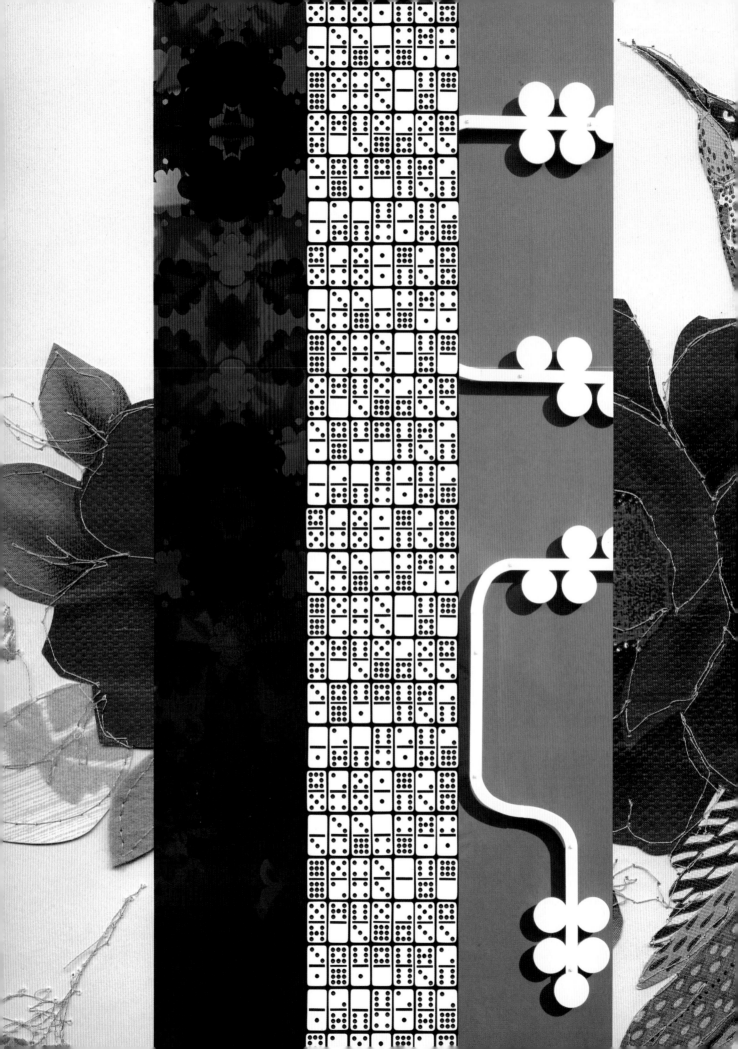

A style that belongs to the recent past is architectural wallpaper; the proliferation of these papers in the 1960s ran parallel to the Modernist post war architecture that was being built in Britain at the time. Many designers were producing papers with large dramatic repeats, to be admired at some distance. Oversized in subject as well as scale, contemporary architectural wallpapers are still very much about expanding our notions of wallpaper and challenging the limitations of production. They are not normally used for domestic spaces, probably because they often have a dominating effect rather than an ambient one. These wallpapers are more often installed in bars, restaurants, clubs and shops to give a dramatic ambiance to a public space and encourage the desired type of customer. Wallpaper has become the signature element in an interiors scheme, to instantly signal where the venue situates itself in terms of clientele. Where once the art chosen and framed would have imparted value and cultural meaning to an interior, wallpaper has achieved enough of an iconic status that it can now accomplish this on its own.

Many of these contemporary architectural designs are graphic or photographic. Their work comes out of the tradition of designers like Fornasetti who used images purloined from books and art and applied them in a surreal way to all sorts of objects, textiles and wallpapers. The designs of Tracy Kendall follow this tradition. She uses photographs of domestic items such as feathers, forks and knives, and turns them back on us as wallpapers. Her papers draw upon the tradition of *trompe l'oeil*, the painter's optical conceit used from the eighteenth century onwards. When one sees Kendall's designs it is almost as if the room has been turned inside out. It is the stuff of everyday life delivered back to us a decorative surface treatment, turning rooms into stage sets on as domestic scale. These papers will instantly make a room look lived in even when it is empty; they give structure where sometimes there is none.

Wallpaper with a three-dimensional aspect to it has also been included in this section. Rather than sitting flush, it takes up the space of the room itself, literally assuming an architectural identity. Ross Neil's *Trees* brings the outside world firmly into the interior. The domestication of nature is highlighted, and the trees infringe upon our space, as we have infringed on theirs.

These wallpapers are in many ways the antithesis of the Bauhaus mentality; rather than stepping back and allowing the architectural shapes of a room to dictate its ambiance, the wallpaper itself does the talking.

# Heather Barnett

Visual artist Heather Barnett explores the point at which art, science, technology and design intersect. Her controversial wallpaper, *Interior Narcissus*, was produced during Barnett's artist residency at Poole Hospital, and uses repeating patterns of magnified cell samples from cervical smears, cheek swabs and blood tests. The micrographs are digitally enhanced so that the colours are boldened and accentuated. At such a large size, the cells appear almost like flowers; the reds, blues and greens merge with one another, in a watercolour swirl, their delicacy highlighting the fine line between beauty and repugnance. Using the human interior in the context of the domestic interior, there is something deeply personal about the way in which the wallpaper exposes the most hidden crannies of our mortality, prompting discussion about the way we perceive our bodies, and challenging the way we select which parts of ourselves to show to the world, and which parts we choose to hide.

*Rooted in Time and Motion* is a further exploration of the interaction between art and science. In this installation, created for the Victoria and Albert Museum in London, seeds were planted in the walls of a garden shed. During the three weeks that the installation was in place, the plants went through their entire life cycle. As they sprouted out of the walls, their roots were pulled down by gravity and the shoots reached upwards, searching for light, creating a surreal dripping of foliage across the walls. The world of nature was brought into a human habitation, and as the plants began to die, the room became a melancholic contemplation of mortality— the room literally came alive, and as the plants began to die, so did the room.

*The Living Room* continued this discussion, incorporating a bed into a similar scenario. This installation raised further questions about mortaliy and the inevitability of fate, calling into question the safety and security of the domestic environments that we inhabit.

1

2

1　*Rooted in Time and Motion*, garden shed installation with cress and mustard seed, grass and inbuilt irrigation system, as part of *The Other Flower Show* at the Victoria and Albert Museum, 2004. Week 1 of the installation.

2　*Rooted in Time and Motion*, Week 5 of the installation.

3, 4　*Rosebud* (magnified graphic of a cervical smear), from the *Interior Narcissus Collection*, developed at Poole Hospital, 2000.

5, 6　*Kaleidoscope* (magnified blood sample), from the *Interior Narcissus Collection*, 2000.

7, 8　*Peach Blossom* (magnified blood sample) from the *Interior Narcissus Collection*, 2000.

Overleaf left:
*Yuletide* (magnified cheek swab), 2000.

Overleaf right:
*The Living Room*, weeks 3 and 4 of the installation at the National Botanic Garden of Wales, 2001.

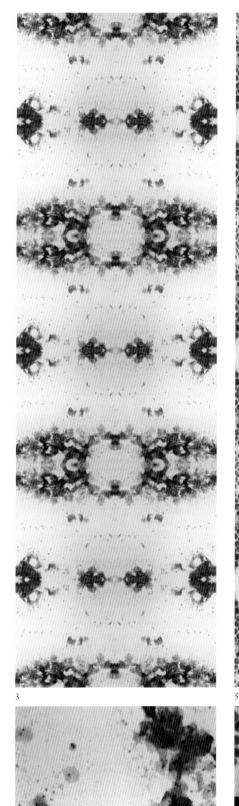

3

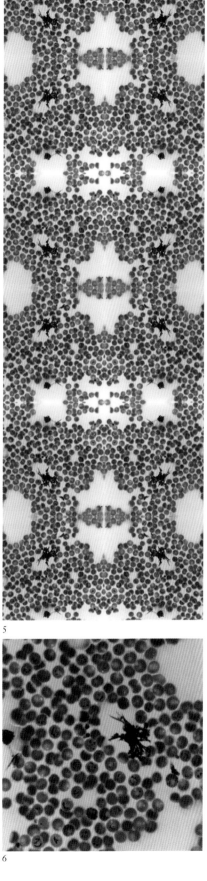

5

7

4

6

8

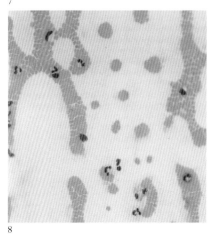

## Susan Bradley

Susan Bradley is a London-based designer
and the creator of *Outdoor Wallpaper*,
a playful and inventive way to bring the
decorative style of the interior into the
unfamiliar and exotic new setting of the
exterior. Traditionally, wallpaper allowed
us to bring elements of the outdoors inside,
using natural, organic shapes taken from
the forms of leaves, ferns and birds, and
transplanting them into the formal habitat
of the house. Bradley has turned this
concept on its head by taking the familiar
forms of wallpaper design, such as damask
and floral motifs, and bringing them back
outside, thereby setting up a fascinating
interplay between the object and its
original inspiration.

Using a variety of materials and finishes
including anodised aluminium, stainless
and powder coated steel, plywood, acrylic
and mirror finish, Bradley's cut-outs have
been installed on buildings and gardens
around the United Kingdom. When the
objects are installed in the ground, they
serve as trellises; the plants climbing up
the man-made materials, accentuating
the differences between the two, and
creating a beautiful juxtaposition of forms.
The 'wallpaper' becomes a living three-
dimensional object—a facilitator for the
plant, rather than a passive emulation.
On larger scale installations on external
walls, the texture of Bradley's work contrasts
with the brickwork, so that it becomes
a decorative element on the canvas of
the wall.

Top and bottom right:
*Damask Outdoor Wallpaper TM*,  installation,
laser cut stainless steel, 2004.

Opposite:
*Vine Outdoor Wallpaper TM*, laser cut stainless steel,
2004. Courtesy of Blue Scooter Photography.

# Clare Coles

Clare Coles' wallpaper boldly merges collage and embroidery with a sheer inventiveness that makes her work totally unique and exciting. Sourcing vintage wallpapers from markets and junk shops, she bypasses the printing process, instead ripping them, stitching wallpapers together, and embellishing them with gems and drawings. The result is a feminine Frankenstein, with the spirit of a butterfly.

Each wallpaper design is brought to life by intricate needlework, which lends her papers a humble delicacy. Depicting beautiful girls, birds and flowers, the sewn panels have an ethereal quality that have the potential to transform their surroundings. Adding leather and felt to the design, she infuses the aged paper with a sleek modernity, and brings them to life with her personalised touch.

Coles has collaborated with other artists and designers on a number of her projects. In *Black Blossom* and *Butterflies*, she worked together with artist Kim Robertson, who created the graphics and the screen-printing, whilst Claire customised the result with stitching and cutting.

Claire Coles is a fine artist as well as a designer. With a background in ceramics, she gradually moved into product design based on the renovation and interpretation of old, unwanted items. Her three-dimensional approach to her products reflects her starting point as a ceramics designer. Some of her products include lampshades made out of wallpaper, and an embroidered table.

1

1  *Kate Dressed Up in Wallpaper*, vintage stitched wallpaper, 2005.
2  *Heather Dressed Up in Wallpaper*, vintage stitched wallpaper, 2006.
3  *Garden Scene*, vintage wallpaper and leather machine-embroidered together, 2004.
4  *Room Scene*, stitched vintage wallpaper, 2004.

Overleaf right:
*Oriental Garden*, leather and felt machine-stitched onto vintage wallpaper, 2006.

Overleaf left:
*Butterfly*, silk-screen printed by Kim Robertson, with vintage wallpaper and leather stitched into the design by Claire Coles, 2005.

2

3

4

# Front

The four women who make up the Swedish design company, Front, met during their degree in industrial design in Stockholm, and much of their work, which is now meeting with enormous publicity, was produced while they were still students. They work as a collective, conducting lengthy discussions about the conceptual realities of the projects they are working on. This collaborative process is very apparent in their work, which positions itself in that blurry hinterland between industrial design and fine art. Their products often communicate a story about the design process, conventions within the field or the material the product is made of.

Their most salubrious project so far has been *Animals*, in which they allowed rats, beetles and other animals to chew their way through wallpaper and other furniture, creating a random pattern that can be aesthetically pleasing or disturbingly violent. The materiality of the paper is brought to the fore, and the role of the designer is brought into question. How can a designer claim ownership if the work was created by an animal?

The randomness of the pattern, which when unrolled resembles a series of Rorschach inkblots, is in keeping with other work by the group. In another example of their work, they replaced the floral motifs of traditional wallpaper with actual flowers bound together and hung from the ceiling in strips. Still other experiments serve to integrate the wallpaper in to the total home environment. *Wallpaper by Shadows* features shadows generated by common household objects physically printed into the paper. Front's wallpaper recasts the modern home not as a shelter from nature and the trials of everyday life but something subject to it and in harmony with it. Wallpaper, and indeed design, is not something controlled and precious for these designers but rather the product of chance and natural variety.

Katja Savstrom, one of the founding members, explains it as follows: "In every design project, a lot of people are involved and there's a random factor. When you are making an object, it won't always turn out the way you wanted it to…. We just wanted to highlight this specific part—the random factor."

1

1    *Tensta Wallpaper*, silk and plastic flowers, mounted onto a white wall. Photography by Anna Lonnerstam and Front.
2, 3  *Design by Sunlight*, a UV sensitive paper, in which the pattern appears when the sun comes out.
4-6  *Rat Wallpaper* from the *Animals* range. Photography by Anna Lonnerstam.

2

3

4

5

6

# Tracy Kendall

London-based wallpaper designer, Tracy Kendall first emerged in 1996 with her two metre high graphic images of blown-up cutlery, flowers and feathers. These magnified monochrome prints recall Man Ray's experiments with the Ray-O-Graph and solarisation. In sharp contrast to this earlier work is Kendall's bespoke range of constructed wallpapers, which defy the notion that wallpapers should *just* be flat against the wall. Adding texture, shadow and depth to a wall, are works such as *In the White Room*, coming out from the backdrop in a mosaic of wallpaper pieces attached by finely stitched thread; and *Flax*, with its carefully hand-cut strands of paper that float out from the wall.

Tracy Kendall treats interiors as muses from which to capture elements that can be reintroduced into the setting, celebrating but also enhancing the natural atmosphere of a room. Working closely with clients, and with the client's belongings, she develops and incorporates them in a way that matches both the room and its inhabitant. This site-specific process precludes her papers from being reproduced for the mass-market.

Kendall claims of her wallpapers that "I want them to convey a strong idea but not to dominate." Her work is about purity, not flashy design. She uses predominantly neutral backgrounds onto which a three-dimensional element is added, subtly evoking the message and original inspiration behind the design.

"Tracy's work is moving in a new direction entirely", says design historian Lesley Jackson, "treating paper more like a textile, weaving it or creating three-dimensional effects by manipulating and involving the paper. That in its own right is completely new."

1

2

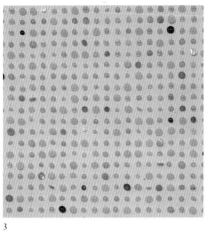

3

4

5

6

7

8

9

10

11

1 Exhibition at Gainsborough studios, wallpaper with mixed media, 2004.
2 *In the White Room*, hand stitched wallpaper with wallpaper hand cut and stitched to it, 2001.
3 *Buttons*, hand-screened, hand stitched with buttons attached with plastic tags, 2003.
4 *Buttons*, detail.
5 *Button Holes*, hand-stitched wallpaper with buttons, 2000.
6 *Cut Close*, hand screen-printed wallpaper, 2005.
7 *Shopping List*, hand-printed wallpaper with printed labels attached with plastic tags, 2002.
8 *Jigsaw*, hand screen-printed wallpaper with jigsaw pieces attached with plastic tags, 2005.
9 *Books*, digital print wallpaper, 2005.
10 *Slim feather*, hand screen-printed wallpaper, 1997.
11 *Fork*, hand screen-printed wallpaper, 1996.

Overleaf left:
*Floral 4*, hand screen-printed wallpaper, 1996.

Overleaf right:
*Florals 2 and 3*, hand screen-printed wallpaper, 1996.

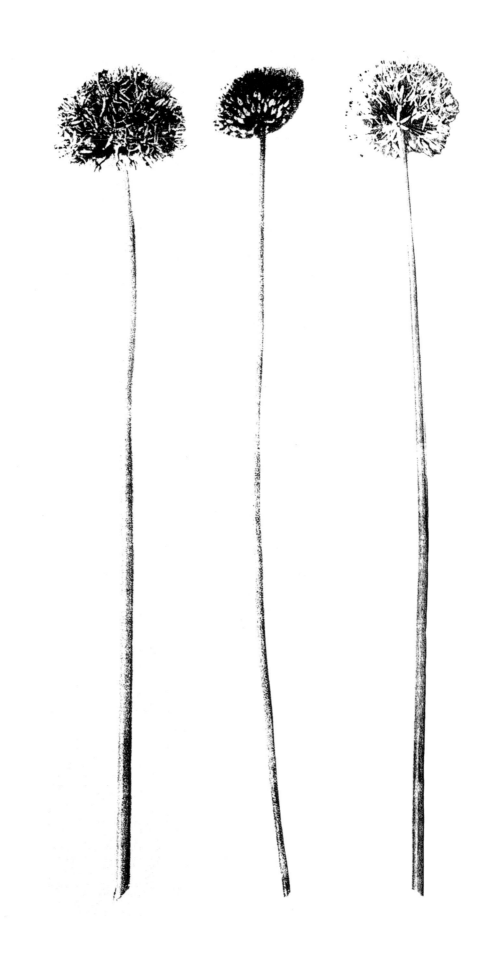

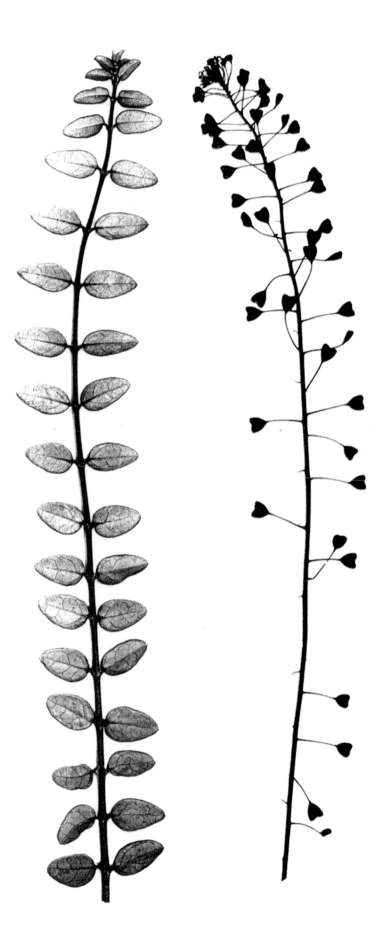

## Ross Neil

Whilst not strictly wallpaper, artist Ross Neil's *Trees* explores the way we interact the space around us, drawing attention to the forgotten corners of a room and turning the wall itself into his canvas. Rather than covering this 'canvas' with paint (or indeed wallpaper), Neil affixes delicate trees to the upper reaches of the wall, and in doing so, turns the whole wall into an upside-down landscape. An audience staring up at the installation can almost suspend their sense of place and feel themselves looking out into a distant forest on the horizon.

The unexpected juxtaposition of exterior and interior, three-dimensional onto two-dimensional, is central to the piece. A person might walk into the room, and suddenly look up and find themselves somewhere else entirely. "My work always has an element of the romantic or surreal about it. I'd like to think my work offers a temporary relief from the day-to-day", says Neil. "Two unrelated objects being thrust together… form a whole other conversation, one that would never have happened otherwise."

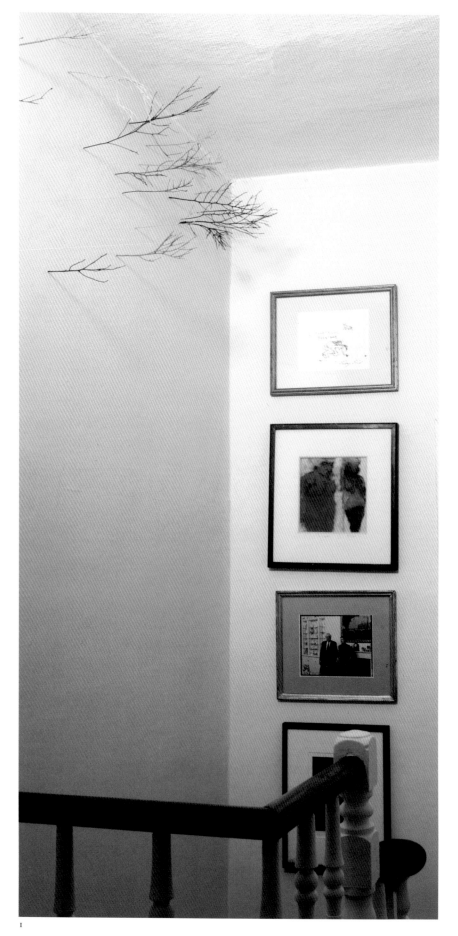

1　*Trees 111* mixed media, dimensions variable, 2006. Photograph by Hugh Kelly, courtesy of Ross Neil.
2, 3　*Trees 11*, dimensions variable, mixed media, collection of Campbell Lutyens, 2006. Photograph by Hugh Kelly, courtesy of Ross Neil.

1

2

3

# Maria Yaschuk

"I am inspired by patterns and textures I see around me and fascinated by the fractured self-similarity of form and the hidden order in the seeming chaos", says Maria Yaschuk of her *Wire Geometrics* collection. This innovative amalgamation of lighting and wallpaper explores the connection and interdependence of physical space and the virtual space created by the surrounding environment.

Playing with light patterns by integrating lighting technologies into wallpaper, Maria Yaschuk's prints create a powerful, majestic and futuristic atmosphere in the interior. They dematerialise the wall space and paint the entire room with their ghostly glow. The patterns of the papers vary. Some are traditional almost damask-like patterns, others are wholly abstract. In *Wall B*, the layering of different patterns and lighting creates an effect that is almost like a human body—the muscles being the solid blues and greens, and the nervous system the fibrous fairy lights that punctuate the design. In *Wall Neon*, a floral effect brings the natural to the realm of the futuristic.

Her interiors, too intense for the average home, are primarily seen in corporate spaces and nightlife spots, where the ultra-modern ambiance speaks of sleek modernity and urban culture. Yaschuk's highly graphic, geometric forms enter into the visual realm of science-fiction and sometimes the conceptual realm of chaos theory, a somewhat unfamiliar territory for wallpaper. Yet this is where her concerns lie: in the latest scientific discoveries and the worlds of tomorrow. Brighter futures indeed.

1

2

1–3 Details from *Wire Geometrics*, 2005.
4, 5 Detail from *Flower Photo*, 2006.
  6 Detail from *Wire Geometrics*.

3

4

5

6

*Interactive*

Whilst wallpapers traditionally come to us printed on a flat roll of paper wrapped in plastic, a new generation of designers are not only challenging accepted design principles, but accepted formats as well. They are producing new textures and encouraging new methods of production, resulting in a much more personalised wallpaper. Jenny Wilkinson takes the idea of paint-by-numbers, and brings it onto the large scale. The pattern is a light and airy outlined design which can be coloured in using paints, coloured pencils or felt tip pens. The designer can choose how much of the pattern to colour in or leave blank, thus dictating the feel of various parts of the room. This is wallpaper that is as much about the idea as the reality. It embraces individuality and turns it into a design notion.

The DIY theme is taken to extremes by designers who ask the customer to make their own wallpapers. The new DIY wallpaper, whether it comprises frames where pictures might be placed, or made from stand-alone stickers that might be combined on the wall, are part of a recent revival of interest in home-decorating crafts among young designers. These emerging styles are emblematic of a renewed interest in having a home-made element to an interior, but broadening the scope of what those elements might be.

The revival of the sticker (or decal as it is known in the United States) has been one of wallpaper's most interesting developments over the past few years. Of course stickers and stencils have been around for a long time but were very much associated with a female aesthetic, falling in line with decoupage and knitting. However, advances in laser-cutting technology have allowed designers to achieve much more complex stickers. British designer Rachel Kelly has worked at the forefront of this trend; fundamental to her work is the notion of creating, or curating, wallpaper *in situ*. Kelly designs patterned and floral stickers that are applied to traditional plain wallpapers, either providing this as a bespoke service or selling packets of her stickers so that people can form their own designs. In a stark deviation from the traditional idea of wallpaper, this controlled DIY provides the design materials but encourages a very personal composition resulting in a sophisticated *haute couture* wallpaper, with no two the same.

Interactive can also apply to digital wallpapers, such as that of Simon Heijdens, who allows the home-owner to dictate the pace and nature of the wallpaper on their walls. Christopher Pearson takes this one step further with his moving Morris-esque designs. His wallpaper is not even tangible but a digital projection on the wall. The wallpaper interacts with the environment surrounding it, and the viewer is therefore forced to interact with the paper itself.

# Antoine et Manuel

Antoine Audiau and Manuel Warosz met whilst studying at art school in Paris, swiftly decided to work together, and have since produced a large amount of distinctive design work together. Since they became a professional pair, they have carved out a characteristic style by combining hand-drawing with computer illustration, and incorporating their own typography and photography into their designs. Their bold, graphic, detailed work has been in demand by fashion designers, publishing houses and even in contemporary dance and theatre, and their unique wallpapers and wall-stickers have adorned the walls of fashionable French buildings and international contemporary art galleries.

Antoine et Manuel's *Possession* wallpaper is a dark, haunting, slightly sinister piece of work, as the name would suggest. It is executed in monochrome, giving it a stark impact, and features black vertical lines that branch off into curious boxes and convolutions, resembling a kind of gothic motherboard. Seen in the context of their other work, a fascination with maps and abstract depictions of places like the Paris Metro map emerges, always twisted and turned into something strange and slightly alien. They have also produced *Possession* wall-stickers in which individual elements of the wallpaper are used as decorative motifs.

Some of their other wall stickers are more innocuous, for example their *Hybrid* and *Tree* designs. The vivid poppy reds and bright lilacs of the *Hybrid* flowers are a million miles from the dark and strange convolutions of *Possession*, but equally are concerned with form and a recurring use of the vertical line to lead the eye and design upwards. Antoine et Manuel love details and silhouettes, and forms unobstructed by shading, dimension or perspective. This can be seen in their *Construction* wallpaper, where everything is seen from the side, as if a cross section had been taken of the scene. The vivid green viaducts interact with tall slender black structures and areas of oozing red, all neatly and perfectly demarcated by crisp white space.

1

2

1  *Possession*, vinyl wall stickers, 2006. Manufactured by Domestic.
2  *Possession Wallpaper*, silkscreen on paper, 2003. Manufactured by Domestic.
3  *Troy*, vinyl wall stickers, 2006. Manufactured by Domestic.
4  *Construction*, installed at the *Unité d'habiation*, digital print, 2006. Manufactured by Domestic.

3

4

## Blik

In this age of the ephemeral and the digital image, it was only a matter of time before the walls of our homes and work would reflect this disposable culture. The Blik decals (in their own words "grown-up's stickers") can be affixed to any flat surface. The results can be dramatic, subtle, humorous and beautiful. In a matter of minutes a blank wall is transformed into a tasteful flock of doves, a frenzy of abstract designs, or a text based tableau of poetry. But these bold statements are by no means permanent. Blik positively encourage stripping the images down at the end of a year, season, week, day—throwaway wallpaper, if you will.

These decals could be seen as an evolution, not of wallpaper, but of wall-printing. Since Victorian times, those who could not afford wallpaper used printing directly on top of walls to create decorative spaces. Without the mess—or the permanence—of potato prints and sponging, Blik's decals afford the DIY-er the freedom to personalise their spaces without committing to a definite design decision. This sense of liberation is also apparent in the designs. *Angels* (a reproduction of an image by artist Keith Haring), *Cloud* and *Fly*, have a lightness and a joy that can provide a refreshing change from traditionally sober designs.

This ingenious self-adhesive enterprise was initiated in 2002 by Scott Flora and Jerinne Neils, now based in Venice, California. In addition to their award-winning retail line of surface graphics, Blik have been commissioned to design and develop wall graphics for both personal and corporate clients.

1  *Angels*, removable, self-adhesive wall decals.
2  *Prose*, removable, self-adhesive wall decals.
3  *Paisley*, removable, self-adhesive wall decals.
4  *Eames*, removable, self-adhesive wall decals.
5  *Cloud*, removable, self-adhesive wall decals.
6  *Fly*, removable, self-adhesive wall decals.
7  *Leaves*, removable, self-adhesive wall decals.
8  *Bounce*, removable, self-adhesive wall decals.

1

"...the mad ones, the ones who are mad to live, mad to talk, mad to be saved, desirous of everything at the same time, the ones who never say a commonplace thing, but burn, burn, burn, like fabulous yellow roman candles exploding like spiders across the stars and in the middle you see th  e  cen   light pop and e   ly  goes Awww!'"
— Jack Kerouac

BLIK 2005

2

3

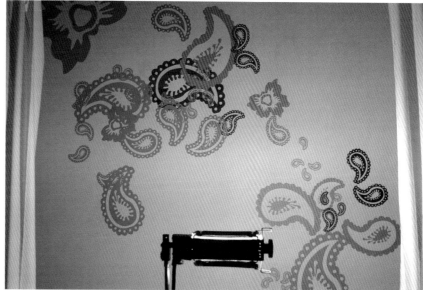

4

5

6

7

8

# Simon Heijdens

Simon Heijdens, a Rotterdam and London-based designer, has produced a new and totally unique product—*Moving Wallpaper*. Rather than a projection on a wall, this is wallpaper that contains within it a pigment that changes colour, in the same way as a Polaroid photograph. This allows the wallpaper to be animated (flowers moving in the wind), switched on and off, or split into a number of different patterns. The wallpaper can work with prepared designs or with any choice of digital or freehand image. You can have wallpaper that depicts (as in the example on the right) flowers for her, and cars for him, or have the two gently morph into one another. The possibilities are endless.

Simon Heijdens has also designed a wallpaper-esque installation simply called *Tree*, which refers to the fact that nature is becoming increasingly rare in The Netherlands, and even organic forms are so regimented that they seem unnatural. An abstract drawing of a tree is projected onto the facade of a building. The tree's leaves and branches move realistically in response to the wind, whilst the leaves drop from their branches if there is a peak in noise levels around the tree. Falling leaves drift until they reach the ground nearby, and as the evening progresses the tree sheds its leaves and becomes increasingly bare, whilst the pavements surrounding become covered in a leaf-fall of light. This beautiful, moving installation is both sentimental and futuristic, it inspires feelings of sadness and longing, and makes a powerful yet poetic statement on the destruction of nature and the relentless progression of urbanisation.

Right:
*Moving Wallpaper*, paper and conductive ink, 2002.

Opposite:
*Tree*, projectors, computers, wind, motion, sound sensors, installed in various locations, 2004.

Overleaf:
*Light Weeds Grow*, 2005.

# Ich&Kar

French graphic art duo, Helena Ichbiah and Piotr Karczewski bring a delicate humour and a distinctly Parisian lightness of touch to their designs. The pair works extensively with wall-stickers, however, rather than assuming a sedate, decorative approach, Ich&Kar, use cartoon-like images that vie for attention in a room. Black cats leap across the wall, stretching seductively just behind a couch in *Catenkit*, and in *Cloudmagic Family*, grey stormclouds with arms and legs bafflingly perform a range of magic tricks.

*Junglepeas* is a little more sedate, but expresses the same unrestrained joy; a fringe of plant fronds is hung from the ceiling of a room, in a way that gently suggests a jungle-like curtain of vegetation, without actually filling the room with such heavy imagery. The *Mytree* design is a tree with human arms for branches. The tree's fruit resemble juggling balls that the hands are keeping in the air. This design literally reaches out to the viewer, inviting them to embrace life in all its hilarity.

These outlandish designs convey a compelling combination of naivete and expressive confidence that is hard to resist. The wallpaper has a dynamism to it that is in direct opposition to the static stability that is usually aspired to in interior design. Rather than turning the home into a sanctuary, they turn rooms into places of inspiration, of energising spirit. The fact that the wallpaper is sold in sticker format offers the homeowner a chance to engage with the playfulness of the content—to share in the joke.

1  *Camouflage Bush*, vinyl wall sticker from the *Vynil* collection, 2005.
2  *Berlingot V-shape*, vinyl wall sticker from the *Vynil* collection, 2005.
3  *Ramy a'louil Heart*, vinyl wall sticker from the *Vynil* collection, 2005.
4  *Cloudmagic Family*, vinyl wall sticker from the *Vynil* collection, 2005.
5  *Mytree*, vinyl wall sticker from the *Vynil* collection, 2005.
6  *Popflower*, in violet, vinyl wall sticker from the *Vynil* collection, 2005.
7  *Boussole*, vinyl wall sticker from the *Vynil* collection, 2005.
8  *Junglepeas*, vinyl wall sticker from the *Vynil* collection, 2005.
9  *Frame*, vinyl wall sticker from the *Vynil* collection, 2006.
10 *Catenkit*, vinyl wall sticker from the *Vynil* collection, 2005.

1

2

3

4

5

6

7

8

9

10

# Rachel Kelly

Rachel Kelly's signature *Interactive Wallpaper* concept is a bespoke wall-covering product. The home-owner selects a background of patterned wallpaper, and then chooses from a selection of stickers that complement or contrast with the base paper. The base papers are delicate prints in an aquarelle palette, whilst the stickers tend to be bold opaque blooms in bright colours, intricately cut out like a lace doily. The overall effect is a layered depth of field that has a dynamism and vibrancy that can bring the room alive.

The home-owner has level of choice in how the room is decorated, and as the stickers are permanent, there is also a degree to which the decorator is allowed to take ownership of the final look. The quirky prettiness is a fun, contemporary interpretation of the traditional floral motif.

A further example of Kelly's whimsical take on design is her *New Shoes* wallpaper, originally commissioned by the sponsors of the cult television series *Sex and the City*. This playful pattern is based on an original, bespoke design, and is available in three colour-ways, amusingly entitled Samantha, Miranda and Charlotte, after the characters in the show. Whilst there is a certain degree of irony in the concept, the design manages to be intelligent and witty as well as achingly feminine, featuring delicate illustrations of designer heels, overlaid on a background pattern of iris flower silhouettes and polka dots.

1

2

1  *Turquoise Branches*, panel installed at the Zetter restaurant in London, 2004.
2  *New Shoes* in Samantha colourway, flexograhphic printed wallpaper, 2005.
3  *Branches*, panel wallpaper in ivory and grey print, hand silk-screen print with stickers, 2004.
4  *Smithfield* (private commission), hand screen print with stickers, 2002.
5  Rachel Kelly installing her work, 2002.
6  *Smithfield* (private commission), hand-screen print with stickers, 2002.

3

5

4

6

## Lene Toni Kjeld

Danish designer Lene Toni Kjeld is another voice pushing wallpaper in new directions. With a background in textile design, Kjeld's work focuses on the way wallpaper defines a space, and has the potential to divide a space. Her paper consists of eight patterns—four main patterns and four hybrids. By using a combination of the patterns and hybrids, her designs can morph as they span the room —lace turning into leaves turning into roses. The decorator can choose where and when these morphologies can occur, defining the feel of specific areas in the room, and lending unique individuality to the overall room design.

Kjeld's background informs the patterns, and there is an awareness of traditional patterning in wallpaper and textiles. *Lace* and *Wave*, for example, show echoes of damask, whereas *Rose* is informed by traditional lace-making techniques. The use of layered patterning and delicate pastel colours gives Kjeld's rooms a historical sensibility— of layers of grandeur that have accumulated over the years, and have rubbed away in places to reveal the beauty and nostalgia of bygone decades. The term 'shabby-chic' isn't quite powerful enough to describe the impact that her fragile designs have on their surroundings.

1

2

3

4

5

6

7

1 *Leaf–Lace*, from the *Wall Decoration*
   collection, 2005.
2 *Lace–Rose*, from the *Wall Decoration*
   collection, 2005.
3 *Lace*, from the *Wall Decoration*
   collection, 2005.
4 *Rose*, from the *Wall Decoration*
   collection, 2005.
5, 7 *Wave–Leaf*, from the *Wall Decoration*
   collection, 2005.
6 *Leaf–Lace*, from the *Wall Decoration*
   collection, 2005.

# Christopher Pearson

Wallpaper designers have always striven
to make their static compositions come alive
with dynamic patterns or suggestions of
narratives, but until Christopher Pearson's
animated wallpaper, movement was only
implied. In Pearson's series *Look at Your
Walls* (a quote taken from William Morris),
he demands the viewer's engagement
with his/her surroundings by projecting
a traditional wallpaper pattern on a wall,
and then manipulating the image with
digital animation.

His most famous piece in this series
is *Willow Boughs*. This is an iconic print by
William Morris, which comprises a very flat
graphic arrangement of branches and leaves.
Pearson's animation sees the piece come
to life; branches naturalistically blowing
in the wind, growing flowers, birds and mice
interacting with the foliage, and the leaves
shrivelling and dying. One particularly
playful sequence shows a nut bouncing
off leaves like a pinball.

Pearson dubs himself a 'digital craftsman',
and aims to strike an emotional rapport with
the user, in the same way that traditional
craftspeople did with hand-blocked prints
in the time of the Arts and Crafts movement.
By using historical prints, and re-interpreting
them, to relate to the twenty-first century,
a certain poetry communicates in a way
that is thoroughly unique. In *Glasgow Toile*,
for example, Pearson animates Timorous
Beasties' ironic re-interpretation of *toile*
prints. The sordid scenes of urban life are
selectively animated so that a seagull is shot,
a building collapses (in reference to the
Gorbals) and a blind man has an accident.
The result is a complex layering of irony
and referencing. Pearson aims to bring
a tangible communicative element to
the digital means that we have at our disposal
today, bridging the gap between technology,
design and art.

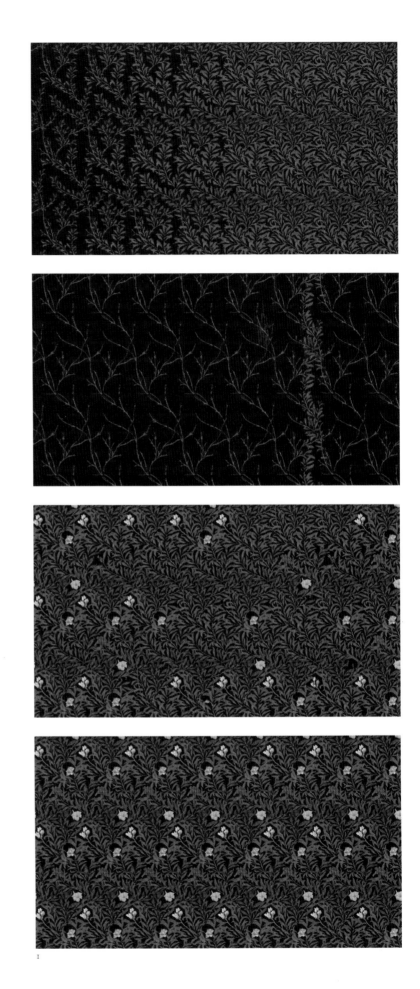

1   Animated frames from *Willow Boughs*
     installation, from the *Look At Your Walls*
     series, 2005.
2   William Morris, *Willow Boughs* original, 1856.

2

# Pepper-mint

In a creative collaboration with traditional wallpaper manufacturer Cole & Son, design house Pepper-mint has come up with a revolutionary new wallpaper called *MagScapes*. This ingenious, magnet receptive wallpaper allows decorative magnetic motifs to adhere to the wall, as if by magic. The concept behind the idea centres on opening up this traditional decorative technique to personal interpretation, and aims to encourage a more playful attitude towards adorning your walls for both children and adults.

Pepper-mint design director, Patricia Adler, is passionate about inventing new ways for people to have fun and interact with their interiors. She is always on the lookout for new ideas that can transform a home whilst inspiring its owner, and believes strongly in encouraging participation in one's own personal space. She says: "Most recently, I have been exploring ways in which wall space may be used for spontaneous creative expression —seeing it as a canvas for anyone's latent-artist." With the invention of *MagScapes*, Pepper-mint have opened up a new arena for playing with your interior in previously undreamt-of ways.

Despite its magnetic properties, *MagScapes* still looks and feels just like an ordinary wallpaper, being light and flexible enough to be hung with paste in the normal way. The responsive, interactive aspect to it points to a new, tactile future for wallpaper, that will surely be developed further.

Right:
*Lily Wallpaper*, from the *MagScapes* range for Cole & Son.

Opposite:
*Metroscapes*, from the *MagScapes* range for Cole & Son.

# Jenny Wilkinson

Jenny Wilkinson made her name in design with her brilliant *Wallpaper-By-Numbers* series. First launched in 2003, these papers are hung like traditional wallpaper but can be coloured in using paint, coloured pencils or felt-tip markers. *Wallpaper-By-Numbers* has been widely heralded as a design classic and is already featured in the permanent collection of the Victoria and Albert Museum in London.

But the series is more than just the execution of a clever idea; the designs themselves reflect her graphic skill and her devilish wit. One pattern seems to simply depict butterflies and flowers, but on closer inspection the innocent flowers turn out to be a forest of predatory venus fly-traps. Another design, which looks like a series of baroque flourishes, actually comprises swimming hammer-head sharks. Often, these humorous touches only reveal themselves after the design has been coloured in and the empty shapes take form. Her imagery often pairs the familiar (puppies and butterflies) with the exotic (tropical plants, and sharks). It is evocative of the distorted world of childhood fantasies.

The beauty of this interactive wallpaper is that the owner is free to disregard Jenny's colour schemes and create a look to match their particular home and style. They can also leave them blank, or half filled in. Naturally, Jenny has also launched a line of *Wallpaper-By-Numbers* catering for children, not just adults reliving their childhood.

1

1　*Venus Flutterby*, screen-print and flexo-roller printed, painted using water based emulsion paints, from the *Wallpaper-By-Numbers* range, 2004.

2　*Tilly*, unpainted from the *Wallpaper-By-Numbers* range, 2003.

3　*Gerbera*, screen-print and flexo-roller printed, half-painted using emulsion paints from the *Wallpaper-By-Numbers* range, 2003.

4　*Tilly*, screen-print and flexo-roller printed, half-coloured, painted using water based emulsion paints from the *Wallpaper-By-Numbers* range, 2003.

5　*Pineapple*, half-painted from the *Wallpaper-By-Numbers* range, 2003.

2

3

4

5

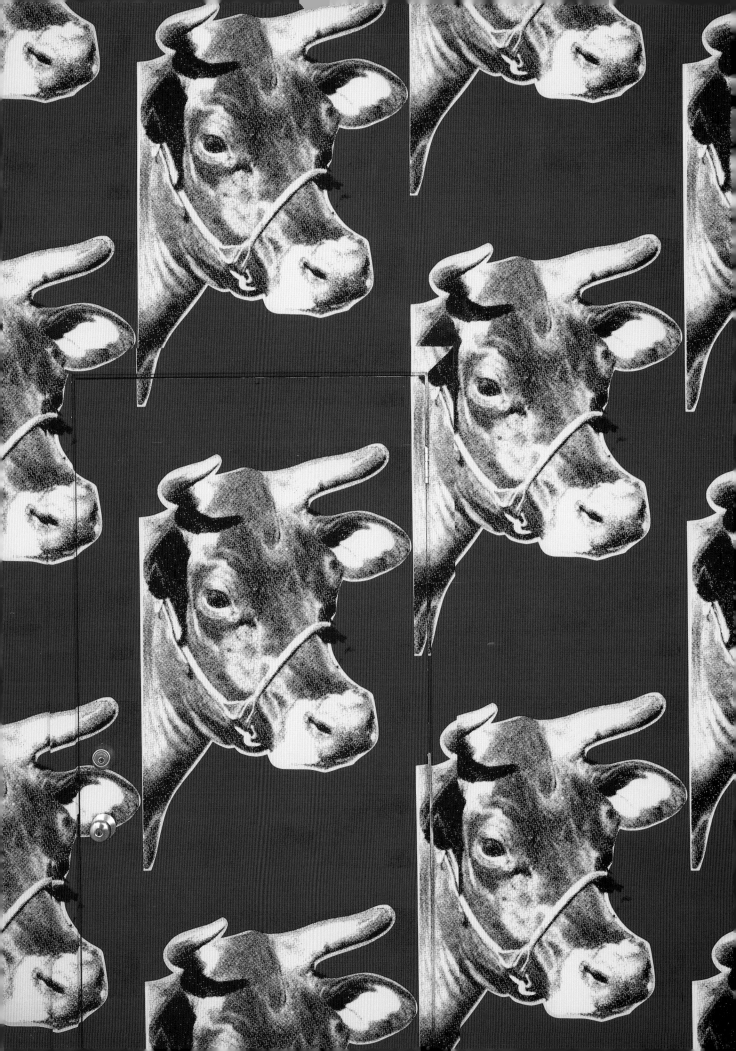

# Wallpaper as Art: A Brief History
## Charles Stuckey

Works executed on walls constitute one of the most ancient and extensive categories of art, extending back some 30 thousand years to images in caves. Even so, wallpaper in art history is seldom addressed.[1] It was not until around 1500 that wallpaper became feasible—as a luxury item—thanks to technological advances in paper production and printing.[2] Although the design of wallpapers has always been artistic, in most cases the status of wallpaper as art has mostly gone unacknowledged since paper wall covering became a common household item after the advent of the Industrial Revolution and mass-production techniques. There are very few surviving wallpapered rooms from before the twentieth century, and visual documentation for art interiors is remarkably scanty.[3]

The rapid growth of museums in the nineteenth century enhanced the status of modern art produced to be collected, but wallpaper, which is manufactured for consumption rather than for preservation, has been at a disadvantage in the museum era. Moreover, due to its sudden widespread availability at low cost around 1850, wallpaper was stigmatised as a commonplace substitute for luxury decor. Of necessity, painters of interior subjects began to include wallpaper backgrounds as a sorry fact of modern life. William Holman Hunt's *The Awakening Conscience*, 1858 (Tate Britain, London), featured a wallpaper showing a cornfield as one among many home furnishings indicative of the moral decay associated with Victorian consumerism. Commenting upon this particular work, John Ruskin condemned such middle-class excesses for their "fatal newness". Presumably, the tawdry wallpaper behind the reclining female in Eduoard Manet's *Olympia*, 1863 (Musée d'Orsay, Paris), served specifically to evoke the vulgarity of a prostitute's love nest. Most often, however, such pioneers of modern painting as Manet and Gustave Courbet, following a seventeenth century Old Master convention, preferred shadowy monochromatic backgrounds for their works with indoor settings.

Negative attitudes about wallpaper were effectively countered by a brilliant modern design arts community based in London, which included Sir Henry Cole, Owen Jones, William Morris, and the artists associated with the Pre-Raphaelite brotherhood. As the name of this group suggests, the Pre-Raphaelites advocated a return to late mediaeval models of surface decoration. They stressed the ancient and universal heritage of elementary patterning, predicated on the capacity of line and colour in the abstract to affect mood. Stimulated by the great international exhibitions of the 1850s and 1860s, the veneration of rhythmic patterns and flat unshaded planes of colour revolutionised the fundamental terms of modern painting in Great Britain. After the Great Exhibition of 1851 in London's Hyde Park with its unveiling of the Crystal Palace, Cole spearheaded efforts to create a museum specifically for the decorative arts. The result was the South Kensington Museum, since 1899 known as the Victoria and Albert Museum.

This London showplace immediately inspired similar institutions in other cities. Although hardly enough to stimulate a competitive market of wallpaper collectors, these decorative arts museums began to form their own study collections of wallpaper samples. More significantly, decorative arts museums endorsed the concept that a room as a whole could deserve consideration as an ambitious work of art. With the exception of art in churches or ceremonial government spaces, there were no venues for the public exhibition of room art until the middle of the nineteenth century; but by 1866, the South Kensington Museum was commissioning rooms as decorative art paradigms, most famously, the wallpapered Green Dining Room by Morris, Marshall, Faulkner, and Co. Such museum acknowledgment bolstered private patronage of artist-designed rooms and encouraged artists to consider an expansion of their traditional specialist roles.

In response to the Pre-Raphaelites' decorative arts activities, expatriate American printmaker and painter James Abbott McNeill Whistler assumed responsibility for creating overall visual environments, such as his famous *Peacock Room*, 1876–77 (now in the Freer Gallery of Art, Washington, DC), commissioned by collector Frederick Leyland, an avid patron of Morris wallpapers. Morris-style wall treatments were antithetical to Whistler's conception of architectural decor, which he derived from so-called Japonism, the far-reaching enthusiasm for Japanese aesthetics after the opening of that isolated country to Westerners in 1855. Essential to Japanese taste was the contrast between decorated and undecorated surfaces. Walls were generally blank. Nonetheless, when Whistler asserted that "the painter [ought to] also make of the wall upon which his work is hung, the room containing it, the whole house, a Harmony, a Symphony, an Arrangement, as perfect as the picture or print which became a part of it,"[4] he was stating an opinion already espoused by Morris. In 1886, Whistler went so far as to wallpaper a London art gallery with plain brown wrapping paper as a chic background for an exhibition of his watercolours and pastels.

Wallpaper design soon captured the imagination of many modern-minded painters in Paris. In his *Grammaire des arts décoratifs. Décoration intérieure de la maison*, 1883, Charles Blanc devoted an entire chapter to wallpaper. Beginning in 1877, Cézanne incorporated wallpaper backgrounds into his still lifes, portraits, and self-portraits, as if to suggest that his own painter's priorities were sympathetic to flat geometric patterning. With reference to Cézanne's *Self Portrait*, 1881, (Tate Modern, London), Meyer Schapiro wrote: "This wedding of the organic [figure] and the geometric has a beautiful simplicity which makes us overlook or accept the arbitrary treatment of the wallpaper pattern. The ornament is not used for surface interest, but as a necessary element of structure in a whole of great concentration and weight."[5]

Paul Gauguin owned a Cézanne still life with a wallpaper background, and in 1890, the younger artist incorporated this into one of his own paintings (now in the Art Institute of Chicago) as background to emphasise the significance of pattern for modern art. As early as 1881, Gauguin had begun including patterned wall coverings as backgrounds in his paintings in order to establish specific moods. For example, the birds represented as background decor in a child's bedroom might suggest flights of imagination. Writing to Vincent van Gogh, Gauguin explained the wallpaper represented in an 1888 self-portrait (Van Gogh Museum, Amsterdam; Vincent van Gogh Foundation); "The girlish background, with its childlike flowers is there to attest to our artistic purity."[6] Van Gogh immediately adopted the wallpaper background concept for his own rather Pre-Raphaelite portraits of members of the Roulin family.

Under the spell of Van Gogh and Gauguin, the young Nabis painters made a veritable cult of decoration in the 1890s.[7] Maurice Denis exhibited wallpaper designs in Paris in 1893, including one arabesque pattern with a railroad train. In his experimental novel *Textes & Opinions du Docteur Faustroll*, 1898, French writer Alfred Jarry, with characteristic humour, has the protagonist take a sponge bath in Denis's train wallpaper! It is possible that Jarry had in mind the sort of contemporary images created by Edouard Vuillard, which incorporate so many different fabrics and wall coverings that the figures all but drown in seas of patterns.

Paintings conceived for ensemble installation (either in terms of shape, colour, or grouping) as a fundamental feature of a particular room were referred to as '*décorations*'. In the opinion of his friends, Claude Monet's paintings made in series (such as the Rouen Cathedral paintings) were foremost *décorations*, ensembles to be exhibited together under ideal circumstances, even if most of them were marketed separately. It is worth mentioning that before the 1895 exhibition of the Rouen Cathedral paintings, a single collector had bought four of them. In addition to such patronage, the example of dealer Samuel Ring's highly publicised Maison de l'Art Nouveau gallery, which opened in December 1895, seemingly prompted Monet to embark upon his famous water-lilies paintings in 1898 specifically as decor for a dining room. By the late 1890s, Bing was commissioning artists such as Henry van de Velde to design model utilitarian rooms for display in his lavish Paris gallery.[8] The rooms, some with wallpaper, may not have been expected to sell as wholes, yet their public display greatly encouraged artist-decorated rooms as entities in themselves.

More and more, as at the 1900 World's Fair in Paris, designer rooms competed for attention at art exhibitions with individual paintings or sculptures, while entire period rooms began to appeal to museums and private collectors. In 1903, the Metropolitan Museum of Art, New York, acquired a room that had been excavated from an ancient villa outside Roman Pompeii; and in 1904, Charles Freer bought Whistler's *Peacock Room* in order to incorporate it into the museum he intended to build in Washington, DC. Before the First World War, whole designer rooms were sometimes included in large contemporary art exhibitions.

Wallpaper permeated the Paris art world by the autumn of 1912, when the controversy over experimental Cubism was at its height. Towards the end of his summer vacation, Georges Braque (who came from a family of housepainters) bought a roll of wallpaper simulating wood paneling and pasted fragments of it into his drawings. Quickly following suit, his friend Pablo Picasso incorporated wallpapers into his own *papiers collées* (collages) no later than October 1913, along with scraps of sheet music and newsprint.[9] True enough, Picasso's Cubism was grounded in the art of Cezanne with its emphasis on patterning as compositional structure; but the wallpaper collage elements in Picasso's works are no more significantly related to Cezanne's paintings with wallpaper than they are to the ongoing Pre-Raphaelite/Nabis cult of pattern so evident in many of Matisse's works beginning around 1908.

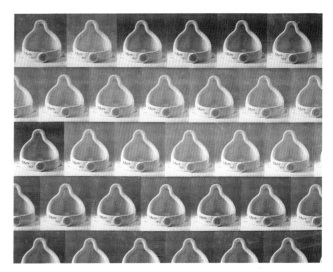

Meanwhile, at the Salon d'Automne of 1912, which opened on 1 October, a group of artists associated with Raymond Duchamp-Villon presented what they called a Cubist House (*La Maison Cubiste*) with framed drawings and paintings installed in a furnished interior with patterned wallpaper. Wallpapered interiors by female designers associated with Paul Poiret's Paris shop, Martine, were also on view in the same exhibition. All of these works seemingly relate to an extraordinary book-object (at least we might call it that today) created at this same time, when Gertrude Stein's privately printed *Portrait of Mabel Dodge at the Villa Curonia*, 1912, was bound in Florentine wallpaper. It is worth noting that Stein may have taken inspiration from her soulmate Alice B Toklas's friend, the San Francisco humourist Gelett Burgess 1866–1951, whose early interviews with Picasso and Braque, are essential to the history of Cubism. In 1896, Burgess used actual wallpaper samples on which to print the text of his satirical single-issue journal *Le Petit journal des Refusés*. Remarkably, Burgess's 1895 poem *The Purple Cow* ("I never saw a purple cow / I never hope to see one...") is sometimes regarded as an inspiration for Andy Warhol's *Cow Wallpaper*. As for the role of wallpaper in classic Cubism, there is no better instance than a 1914 *Still Life* (Museum Ludwig, Cologne) by the Russian artist Liubov Popova, which prominently includes the letters 'WALLPA'. Popova came to Paris to study modern art in November 1912.

Despite the advocacy of Picasso and Matisse regarding surface pattern, after the First World War, the very idea of wallpaper became antithetical to Modernist style, based primarily on the spare Arts and Crafts attitude of Frank Lloyd Wright and its heritage in the ascetic interiors of the de Stijl movement, the Bauhaus, and International Style designers and architects. Increasingly, the thoughtful up-to-date display of paintings and sculpture became predicated on neutral white walls with as little ornamentation as possible.

Some notable painters designed wallpapers for commercial manufacture during the Art Deco years; among them, Raoul Dufy, Charles Burchfield, Rene Magritte, and even Joseph

View of two burnt drawings installed on gallery walls, *Obsessive Compulsive* and *Oops!*, burnt paper, Sintra board, paint, acrylic bushings, screws, magnets, 2005, by Jane Masters.

Top:
*Reward*, 2005
by Michael Mercil.

Above:
*In my Father's House*,
installed at the
University of Virgina,
2000, by Michael
Mercil.

Cornell. Still, they tended to keep their careers as painters separate from their decorative-art projects. After Cubism, references to wallpaper in paintings tended to be satirical, aimed at the old-fashioned vulgarity of middle-class taste. Marcel Duchamp's assisted 'readymade', *Apolinère Enameled*, 1916–1917 (Philadelphia Museum of Art), shows a wallpapered interior with a girl in the process of making her own 'readymade', transforming a dated bedstead by painting it. In the 1930s, when Duchamp acted as interior decorator for his companion Mary Reynolds, he pasted maps all over a wall of her Paris apartment instead of using ordinary wallpaper. As if to appeal to any and every taste in interiors, Francis Picabia in 1919 transformed an empty frame into an assemblage, the *Danse de Saint Guy* (Centre Georges Pompidou, Paris) by stretching a few strings across it. Visible as a result of the object's openness, any wall on which this artwork is displayed becomes incorporated into it, just as the surrounding or underlying decor inevitably appears in works by Picabia's friends, whether observed through the transparent surfaces of Duchamp's works in glass or the reflective surfaces of Brancusi's polished bronzes.

Coincidentally, the integration of art and room in these highly unconventional works paralleled the heyday for the acquisition of period rooms by museums in the 1920s, ranging historically from ancient times to the present. In the opinion of Museum of Modern Art director Alfred Barr, "probably the most famous single room of twentieth century art in the world" was El Lissitsky's 1927–1928 *Abstract Cabinet*, commissioned by the Landesmuseum in Hannover. Lázsló Moholy-Nagy would also create a room for the same art museum in 1930.[10] The Musée Claude Monet, opened at the Orangerie in Paris in 1927, consisted of two oval rooms designed specifically for the artist's *Nymphéas (Water Lilies)* murals, which were glued to the walls to make removal impossible. Not intended for any function or ceremony whatsoever, these are probably the first public spaces ever established exclusively for art reverie.

Such spaces have proliferated since the end of the Second World War. In response to the exhibition of assertive and demanding five metre wide paintings by Jackson Pollock, Barnett Newman, and Clyfford Still at the Betty Parsons Gallery, New York, around 1950, an enthusiasm developed for wall-to-wall, floor-to-ceiling, and even wrap-around-the-room artworks, all with inevitable wallpaper overtones. Famously, critic Harold Rosenberg in 1952 referred to large Abstract Expressionist paintings as "apocalyptic wallpaper".[11]

Around that time, it was Rene Magritte who most specifically addressed the wallpaper-as-art concept. He had included patterned wallpapers as bourgeois background in *The Pebble*, 1948 (Musees Royaux des Beaux-Arts de Belgique, Brussels), and *The Survivor*, 1950 (The Menil Collection, Houston); and in 1958, he completed his most ambitious mural decoration for the Casino in Knokke-le-Zoute, the eight panels of which have backgrounds of clouds, curtains, or wallpaper patterning. Themes of interior decoration took on special significance in his conventional easel paintings around this time. In several, he repeated unit images (a man in a bowler hat or a loaf of French bread, for example) wallpaper-wise at equal intervals, thus demonstrating the sublimity of repetition and pattern in surreal fashion. Other paintings showed strange interior walls made of living rock or sky. The room depicted in *Personal Values*, 1952 (Museum of Modern Art, San Francisco), has walls decorated with clouds on blue, as if they were made of glass, revealing the outside sky surrounding some isolated skyscraper's heavenly upper floor.

During the 1950s, several artists who had nothing the least to do with wallpaper nevertheless stressed the walls of the display room in an unprecedented way, thus initiating what is today called installation art. In the late 1950s and 60s, such work was more often referred to as an 'environment,' and with some justification, Louise Nevelson credited herself with inventing the genre. Given the scale and complexity of her wall-hugging pieces, however, they seldom appear in museum surveys highlighting that time period. In this context, it would be wrong not to mention Yves Klein's *Le Vide*, presented at the Galerie Iris Clert, Paris, in 1958. Having painted over the gallery windows with his hallmark blue, Klein otherwise left the walls bare—an empty room filled with priceless nothing to sell or to possess.

Wallpaper itself did play a part in work by some of the artists who pursued the creation of "environments" and room art in the late 1950s and early 60s. Edward Kienholz's *Roxy's* (Collection Reinhold Onnasch, Berlin) was exhibited at the Alexander Iolas Gallery, New York, in 1963. Kienholz included walls separate from those of the gallery in this life-size evocation of a Nevada whorehouse, complete with tacky wallpaper. Around 1964, James Rosenquist used patterned paint rollers to imprint several of his complex Pop masterpieces with wallpaper patterns, including *Lanai*, 1964 (ex-collection John and Kimiko Powers).

As if in response to recent works by Kienholz, Rosenquist, and others, as well as to the Museum of Modern Art's 1960 exhibition of Monet's works in series, Andy Warhol brought wallpaper into its own in 1966 with an April exhibition at the Leo Castelli Gallery, New York. Warhol presented a room hung all around with his *Cow Wallpaper*. The space contained nothing else, effectively extending Klein's idea of a commercial exhibition with no art for sale. Although they were little more than relics of Warhol's masterpiece environment, clients could purchase rolls of the printed paper, just as they might collect an unframed print for display. Warhol signed somewhere around 100–150 wallpaper samples.

Sadly, no patron ever came forward to acquire the unforgettable work on its own terms, whatever they might be understood to be.[12] Never mind that Warhol had opted to hand over the production process to a commercial fabricator. Since this wallpapered room would be destroyed upon de-installation, how could it be handled as art for the market or museum? Could a collector stockpile enough extra rolls of the *Cow Wallpaper* to ensure its availability as needed forever? Storage and re-installation problems aside, was the work as a whole conceived as something unique or as something more like an unlimited edition available to anyone purchasing sufficient rolls of wallpaper for future use? First acclaimed as an advertising artist, Warhol seemed determined to eradicate the distinctions between 'commercial' art and 'museum' art after he began to make paintings and sculptures for gallery display around 1960. To this end he created paintings of everyday items bearing images: dollar bills, comics, newspapers and magazines, merchandise packaging, and so on. His *Cow Wallpaper* is just this sort of product, except that its prestige was considerably enhanced upon display as the 'content' of an art-gallery exhibition. In truth, Warhol's wallpaper would look as out-of-place in a home as in a gallery. With its garish colours and simple reiterated motif, the printed paper little resembles a professionally designed product, relating instead to 1960s Warhol prints showing nearly identical sequential images from rolls of motion-picture film (by this time Warhol was making his own underground movies). Warhol eventually used *Cow Wallpaper* in its traditional role as a background for the display of his own paintings, but as presented in 1966, it was a background become foreground. It could also be considered an absurdist theatre setting *a la* Alfred Jarry awaiting the arrival of its cast of characters, a sort of Pop Happening with the gallery visitors as unwitting performers.

One of the hallmarks of 1960s New York art was the integration of the display wall as a component in many large works. This is the case with the light-bulb sculptures that Dan Flavin began to make in 1968 (*alternate diagonals of March 2, 1964*, consisting of red and yellow bulbs, thus in part anticipating Warhol's *Cow Wallpaper*).[13] William Anastasi took the wall to task in a variety of 1966 works exhibited the following year at Dwan Gallery, New York. Notable among them are *Trespass*, the meticulous removal of a section of the paper skin of the gallery's Sheetrock wall; and *Six Sites*, photographic images of the gallery walls silkscreened at 9:10 scale onto canvases installed on the very walls they represent. Gordon Matta-Clark had a similar interest in deconstructing walls, not to mention buildings, and documenting it artistically. In 1972, Matta-Clark created an installation entitled *Wallspaper* at the 112 Greene Street gallery, and the following year he published an artist's book of photographed wallpaper from a tenement undergoing demolition.

Sol LeWitt's drawings, first exhibited in 1969 at the Paula Cooper Gallery, New York, were the climax of such works. Covering the entire wall as wallpaper would, these are to be realised by any draftsperson according to the artist's written description, such as: *Wall Drawing 358: A 73" (30 cm) Grid Covering the Wall. Within Each 12" (30 cm) Square, One Arc from the Corner. (The direction of the arcs and their placement*

*Bullies*, fluorescent flocked wallpaper, blacklights and wooden locker room bench. Installation exhibited in *Apocalyptic Wallpaper* group exhibition, Wexner Center for the Arts, Columbus, Ohio, 1997 (originally 1992), Virigil Marti. Photograph by Richard K Loesch.

*are determined by the draftsman).* By relinquishing personal responsibility for the physical execution of these works, LeWitt overcame the drawbacks of traditional wallpaper art. The work's owner might remove, store, and reinstall any wall drawing with relatively few complications, since all that is needed are the instructions. Each new incarnation would be slightly different, as each performance of a musical score is uniquely expressive of the interpretative capacities of the performers, yet it remains the composer's art.

Emerging West Coast conceptual artist John Baldessari immediately seized upon the absurd humour of the situation. In 1971, Baldessari instructed students at the Nova Scotia College of Art and Design to cover a gallery's walls with the phrase, "I will not make any more boring art." Partly a respectful parody of LeWitt's deadpan written instructions for the generation of artworks by assistants, Baldessari's work is also a satirical commentary on the sorts of language art applied directly to gallery walls by Mel Bochner, Joseph Kossuth, Lawrence Wiener, and many others beginning in the mid-1960s. In 2000, Baldessari finally realised *"I Will Not Make Any More Boring Art"* as actual wallpaper.

Wall and wallpaper art have had a wide variety of embodiments worldwide, starting no later than 1959, when Austrian painter Friedrich Hundertwasser and his collaborators covered the walls of the Hamburg art school with an endless spiral. In Paris at the Salon de lajeune peinture in 1967, Daniel Buren, Olivier Mosset, Michel Parmentier, and Niele Toroni presented works with the sort of simple patterning more familiar in wallpaper than painting. With characteristic paradox, Buren sought to present such objects made from a particular striped awning material without reference to walls. The so-called BMPT group (an acronym based on the initials of their names) immediately gave license to Claude Viallet and the Support-Surface group, whose simply patterned works without stretchers must be taken into consideration in any brief survey of wallpaper-related art.

*Untitled*, (Turbinenhalle), individually coloured linen fabric in 96 different colors, glazed clay tiles, installed in the Turbine-Hall of the Stadwerke Dusseldorf, 2003, by Jorge Pardo.

Warhol's underground films and the experimental ways of projecting them seemingly encouraged such pioneering artists as Michael Heizer and Dennis Oppenheim. By no later than 1970, they began to exhibit environments of what might be called 'projected wallpaper', using photographs, film loops, or videotape to produce wall-scale images.[14] Such projected wall/wallpaper art took on futuristic overtones around 1990 with the advent of cyberspace and home computers. Not by chance, the wealth of screensaver graphics for computer monitors in rest mode are called 'wallpapers'. Monumental video "wallpapers" consisting of hundreds of adjacent video screens now often dominate festival venues and corporate commercial displays from the Seoul Olympic Games to the Venice Biennale. Of course, the most brilliant advocate of this new public art type is Nam June Paik. Increasingly, blockbuster films such as *The Matrix Reloaded*, 2003, incorporate wall displays as originated by Paik to symbolise

a brave new technological world with a constant kaleidoscopic panorama of background images.

Issues of technological decor and Pre-Raphaelite pattern aside, the most important wallpaper art of the last 25 years deals with background as moral statement. Adrian Piper made a 1977 installation consisting of a small room (1 × 1.5 × 2 metres) wallpapered with photographic images of racial suffering stamped over with the words 'Not A Performance'. A spectator taking a seat in this environment, entitled *Art for the Artworld, Surface Pattern*, 1977 (private collection), is temporarily imprisoned with his/her awareness of ongoing social injustice.

Piper's intense room set an important precedent for many memorable wallpaper-art pieces. Perhaps best known is the 1988 AIDS environment wallpapered with AIDS posters by General Idea. Alluding to Robert Indiana's famous LOVE painting 1966 (Indianapolis Museum of Art), General Idea created a bold pattern of the acronym for Acquired Immune Deficiency Syndrome, thus proposing that it should be both fashionable and compellingly necessary to address the most challenging horrors of our times. Associations of unobtrusive domestic comfort notwithstanding, wallpaper has the capacity to make any message numbingly present.

In 1989, Robert Gober began to use similar politically charged wallpaper components in his installations, starting with *Male and Female Genital Wallpaper* and *Hanging Man/Sleeping Man*, both predicated on the need to confront taboo issues that define self and other in our society. The sort of repetition inherent in wallpaper design is most often associated with boredom, but in works by General Idea, Gober, Marti, and Piper, the multiplication of ominous images is riveting, no matter how painful. Marti has transformed wallpaper into a medium of gothic self-awareness by framing sweet-seeming photographic images of boys as poisonous flowers of evil in his *Bullies* wall covering of 1992. More recently, the long-standing notion that wallpaper adds warmth to domestic settings has been questioned by a growing number of younger artists. Christine Tarkowski makes dot designs on wallpaper sheets by shooting bullets through them.

Now, at the outset of the twenty-first century, wallpaper art has become ubiquitous in our propagandistic marketing culture. Reporting on messages such as 'Strengthening Our Economy' that appear as surface-design pattern backdrops to underline the message of every political speech, *Time* magazine stated last July that the American government has "made a habit of visual message bearing, regularly wallpapering the President's backdrop with the official theme of the day".[15] In art and in public life, twenty-first century scale is intended to be all encompassing, wall-to-wall and floor-to-ceiling, like wallpaper.

Reprinted courtesy of Charles F. Stuckey; Museum of Art, Rhode Island School of Design, Providence, USA; and the Fabric Workshop and Museum, Philadelphia, USA; from Charles Stuckey, "Wallpaper As Art: A Brief History," in Judith Tannenbaum and Marion Boulton Stroud, *On The Wall: Contemporary Wallpaper*. Providence: 2003, pp. 35–49.

1   Hapgood, Marilyn Oliver, *Wallpaper and the Artist, From Dürer to Warhol*, New York: Abbeville Press Inc., U.S.A, 1992.

2   Hoskins, Lesley, ed., *The Papered Wall: History, Pattern, Technique*, London: Thames and Hudson, 1994.

3   For a survey of the documentation see Mario Praz, *An Illustrated History of Interior Decoration from Pompeii to Art Nouveau*, London: Thames and Hudson, 1964 (ed. 1982); and Charlotte Gere, *Nineteenth Century Decoration: The Art of the Interior*, New York: Harry N Abrams, 1989.

4   Quoted in Joseph Mascheck, "The Carpet Paradigm: Critical Prolegomena to a Theory of Flatness", *Arts*, vol. 51, no. 1, September 1976, pp. 82–109.

5   Schapiro, Meyer, *Paul Cézanne*, New York: Harry N Abrams, 1963, p. 52.

6   Quoted in Richard Brettell, *The Art of Paul Gauguin*, Washington, DC: National Gallery of Art, 1988, p. 33.

7   See Gloria Groom, *Beyond the Easel: Decorative Paintings by Bonnard, Vuillard, Denis and Roussel, 1890–1930*, Chicago: Yale University Press, 2001.

8   Weisberg, Garbrei, *Art Nouveau Bing: Paris Style 1900*, New York: Abrams, 1986.

9   Richardson, John, *A Life of Picasso, Volume II: 1907–1917*, New York: Pimlico, 1996, pp. 60, 249. See Elizabeth Cowling, *Picasso, Style and Meaning*, London: Phaidon Press, 2002, pp. 240–53; and Nancy J Troy, *Modernism and the Decorative Arts in France, Art Nouveau to Le Corbusier*, New Haven and London: Yale University Press, 1991, passim.

10  Staniszewski, Mary Anne, *The Power of Display: A History of Exhibition Installations at the Museum of Modern Art*, Cambridge, MA and London: MIT Press, 1998, pp. 16–21.

11  See Donna M De Salvo, *Apocalyptic Wallpapers: Robert Gober, Abigail Lane, Virgil Marti and Andy Warhol*, Columbus, Ohio: Wexner Centre for the Arts, Ohio State University, 1997, pp. 8 and 13.

12  Not counting Holly Solomon. In 1966, she wanted Andy Warhol to use a photograph of herself (rather than the cow design) to make a wallpaper for her home. As a dealer, Solomon would subsequently specialise in Pattern and Decoration artists. Perhaps inadvertently, but certainly ironically, her book *Living with Art*, 1988, authored with Alexandra Anderson, documents how taboo wallpaper remains in contemporary interiors. There is none visible in any of the rooms represented in her survey of collectors' homes.

13  For an overview of the genre, see Jörg Schellmann, ed., *Wallworks, Site-specific Wall Installations*, Munich: Edition Schellmann, 1999.

14  See Chrissie Iles, *Into the Light, The Projected Image in American Art 1964–1977*, New York: Harry N Abrams, 2001.

15  "Watch His Back" in *Time*, vol. 160, no. 5, 29 July 2002, p.15.

## Selected Bibliography

Atterbury, Paul and Clive Wainwright eds, *Pugin: a Gothic Passion*, New Haven and London: Yale University Press in association with The Victoria and Albert Museum, 1994.

Bosker, G, and L Lencek, *Off the Wall: Wonderful Wall Coverings of the Twentieth Century*, San Francisco: Chronicle Books, 2003

Clark, Jane Gordon, *Wallpaper in Decoration*, London: Francis Lincoln Ltd, 2001.

De Salvo, Donna M, *Apocalyptic Wallpapers: Robert Gober, Abigail Lane, Virgil Marti and Andy Warhol*, Columbus, Ohio: Wexner Centre for the Arts, Ohio State University, 1997.

Gere, Charlotte, *Nineteenth Century Decoration: The Art of the Interior*, New York: Harry N Abrams, 1989.

Hapgood, Marilyn Oliver, *Wallpaper and the Artist, From Dürer to Warhol*, New York: Abbeville Press Inc., USA, 1992.

Hoskins, Lesley ed., *The Papered Wall*, London: Thames and Hudson, 1994.

Jackson, Lesley *'Contemporary': Architecture and Interiors of the 1950s*, London: Phaidon, 1994.

Jackson, Lesley, *Twentieth Century Pattern Design*, New Jersey: Princeton Architectural Press, 2002.

Parry, Linda ed., *William Morris*, London: Philip Wilson Publishers in association with The Victoria and Albert Museum, 1996.

Praz, Mario, *An Illustrated History of Interior Decoration from Pompeii to Art Nouveau*, London: Thames and Hudson, 1964 (ed. 1982).

Pugin, AWN, *The True Principles of Pointed or Christian Architecture*, London: John Weale, 1841.

Saunders, Jill, *Wallpaper in Interior Decoration*, London: V&A Publications, 2002.

Schellmann, Jorg ed., *Wallworks, Site-specific Wall Installations*, Munich: Edition Schellmann, 1999.

Sebba, Anne, *Laura Ashley: a Life by Design*, London: Weidenfeld & Nicolson, 1990.

Sherman, Margaret ed., *Daily Mail Ideal Home Book 1951–2*, London Associated Newspapers Ltd, 1951.

Singsen, Judith A ed., *On The Wall: Contemporary Wallpaper*, Rhode Island and Philidelphia: Rhode Island School of Design and The Fabric Workshop and Museum, 2003.

Troy, Nancy J, *Modernism and the Decorative Arts in France, Art Nouveau to Le Corbusier*, New Haven and London: Yale University Press, 1991.

Turner M, M Pinney and L Hoskins, *A Popular Art: British Wallpapers 1930–1960*, London, 1989.

Whately Alice, *Modern Wallpaper & Wallcoverings: Introducing Color, Pattern and Texture Into Your Living Space*, New York, 2002.

## Acknowledgements

This book would not have been possible without the dedication and commitment of all the people involved. Thanks first and foremost to the wallpaper artists and designers who provided images and information. Their patience and generosity is greatly appreciated.

Holly Pester, Kat Kowaleska and Dave Moats, for their research assistance and for writing up the designer profiles.

Anjana Janardhan for early research on the project.

Philip Toledano, Laurie McGahey and Alex Sadvari at The Fabric Workshop and Museum, for their time and assistance with picture research.

Judith Singsen and Judith Tannenbaum at Rhode Island School of Design, for permitting us to use the Charles Stuckey essay.

Silvia Sokalski at Bruno Bischogberg Gallery.

Jeffrey Cheung and Kirsty Philip at Habitat, Cristina at IKEA, Loreta Prestia at Laura Ashley, Susan Wilks at Llewelyn-Bowen Ltd, Olivia Plunkett at *Wallpaper\**, Greg Burchard at the Warhol Museum, for their help with images.

Anna Cole at Blow.

Essays by Timothy Brittain-Catlin, Jane Audas and Charles Stuckey
Edited by Cigalle Hanaor
Assistant Editor, Blanche Craig
Profile texts by Holly Pester, Katherine Kowaleska and David Moats
Design by John Morgan Studio, London

Black Dog Publishing Limited
Unit 4.4 Tea Building
56 Shoreditch High Street
London
E1 6JJ

Tel: +44 (0)20 7613 1922
Fax: +44 (0)20 7613 1944
Email: info@bdp.demon.co.uk

www.bdpworld.com

ISBN 10: 1 904772 56 0
ISBN 13: 978 1 904772 56 9